WELLNESS FOR SUPER-SENIORS

*How to Support Your Parents' Health & Happiness
& Help Them Live Longer Better*

SUPER-SENIOR HEALTH GUIDE

JUAN O'CALLAHAN

TO THE MEMORY OF FRANK

My friend, mentor, and inspiration

ACKNOWLEDGEMENTS

I owe a debt of gratitude to the many students in my classes who helped me develop this project, and to the physicians who lectured to my students; also, for the innumerable hours spent by my editor and copy editor, Muireann and Maria O'Callaghan. I gained valuable insights from the critiques of two professional coaches, Bruce McAllister and Lisa Tener (alas, I have not followed all of their instructions, otherwise this would be a better book). And thanks to the many others who have helped, especially my webmaster Robert Neve and my assistant instructors Paul Janssens and Robert Evans. Last, but not least, to my wife Bunny who encouraged me to follow my dreams and do what I do well; not only well, perhaps, but better.

TABLE OF CONTENTS

FOREWORD

This book is a three-part tome: it's a story, a how-to fitness manual, and a cookbook.

The early chapters of "my story" explain why this complete wellness program is important to both you and to your elderly parents' health and happiness.

If you want to skip or skim the story narrative and some of the rationale, go directly to the exercise and nutrition sections, chapters 4, 5, 8, and 9. They are self-explanatory, easy to teach and/or perform, and you will find that they are not only beneficial for your super-senior parent/s (in their late-70's or 80's or 90's)—they will change your own lifestyle.

When you return to read "the story" sections, you'll find a compelling raison d'être why so many super-seniors (and some of their children) who follow this regimen are committed to living their lives, not only longer, but also better.

My theme is inclusion when it comes to aging: inclusion of all aspects of fitness, nutrition, and awareness; and inclusion of the whole family. In deciding to address this book primarily to the children of super-seniors, I did not intend being condescending in tone toward super-seniors. I am a super-senior. Yes, I might feel somewhat put out if I came across a manual telling my children how to care for me. But the reason this wellness guide for super-seniors is written—in the main—for our younger offspring and caregivers is that they are the ones who most often choose to be our advocates in later years when we are "ultra-seniors." If they help and encourage us now—right now—they (and we) will have an easier time of living better in the decades ahead.

Juan O'Callahan

Stonington, CT

September, 2012

Chapter 1.

Why Your Parents Need The Super-Senior Health Guide

Now, Not Later

I don't need physical or life-planning help from my children, yet. But I may in a decade. I'm just going on eighty. I've been lucky in that another person set me on the path to better health when I was in my mid-fifties. If that had not happened, I would not be presenting the Super-Senior Health Guide to you, and you would not be reading this book—*Wellness For Super-Seniors*—for I surely would have died quite young.

Suffice it to say, I was not a good example to my peers or those who were a few years older at the time. They, for the most part, undoubtedly led calmer and less self-destructive lives. They are the men and women who have now reached the eighties and nineties and they are your parents.

Even though those good folk were fairly active and seemingly healthy in the years before retirement, many may have let their guard down after that. They may have become more passive, even sedentary, gained a little weight and girth, and slipped into a lower gear during their early-seventies. It happens to a lot of us, the imperceptible slide to slowdown. For some, that's fine—certain super-seniors thrive on the quieter lifestyle, their physical appearance or gait does not change, and they don't have medical issues that require multiple prescription drugs.

But others—those in their late-seventies who, like me, are entering the eighties, and especially men and women in their early-nineties—may be experiencing the consequences of habits that were essentially set in place ten or fifteen years earlier.

We in America—and, indeed, in all so-called first-world "developed" nations—have, by and large, achieved standards of affluence that unfortunately foster lethargy, a sedentary lifestyle, excess weight and girth, anxiety and irritability, some or all of which lead to potentially-avoidable yet serious, late-in-life illnesses.

Most of today's super-seniors are living far, far longer than your great-grandparents did—thirty years longer, in fact—*but not necessarily better.* As the children of the twenty million over-75's super-seniors in this country, many of you will be looking for a new, total wellness game plan for them. Even if one or both of your parents have moved from their own home to a retirement community, or to an assisted-living or nursing home, or retained a part-time caregiver or visiting nurse, there is often the need for yet something else: something to give more meaning to their lives.

That's where my *Wellness For Super-Seniors*—the SSHG Super-Senior Health Guide—fits in and can play a distinct and special role in the revitalization of your loved one, whether a parent, a cousin or uncle, or a lifelong older friend.

I have a cousin who is 89 and I have been her guardian, caregiver, power-of-attorney, and dear friend for the past ten years. If I had not "adopted" her and taken on the challenge of her health and welfare a decade ago, even though she might have been ensconced in a qualified nursing home, she and I both know that she would have died long since. I applied the three pillars of my *Wellness For Super-Seniors* to her life, coerced her into exercising, eating better, understanding her medications, being interested in others, and regaling me with memories of her youth and stories of our family.

I teach fitness and nutrition classes for over-75's in several locations, and one of my earliest students, Helane, is a 93-year-old, long-retired small-business owner. Helane's daughter initially brought her to my class and continues to do so twice a week. Her daughter, Janet, wrote to a friend recently in regard to her friend's father—with a copy to me—and her poignant words make the efforts that I expend worthwhile:

> The class regime of Juan's isometric and aerobic exercises
> is designed specifically for women and men aged 75 to

100. I think my mom has been attending Juan's classes for close to four years. She joyfully looks forward to each class and to see Roxanne (another student), the guardian angel who is waiting at the doorway to escort her and your father safely inside.

In addition to improving balance and strength and learning about healthy eating, the SSHG is much about camaraderie and getting renewed pleasure out of living; living *better* in fact.

Wellness For Super-Seniors sets out some of the essential "tools" for revitalization of our oldest population group, for your parents—if they need it. These tools are designed to help guide super-seniors on living those extra 20 to 30 years with a sense of happiness and healthy functioning.

Super-seniors, who may not be quite as healthy as they would like to be, will more successfully start a new lifestyle program entailing wellbeing and renewed vitality through the help and interaction of their adult children (technically seniors themselves) or other relatives, or through the persuasion of a caregiver or close friend—perhaps even at the instigation of a spouse who happens to be healthier or younger. Introduction, encouragement, and constant, gentle persuasion are keys.

In helping super-seniors over the years improve their general wellness through my SSHG regimen, I've seen the important role adult children—men and women in their fifties and sixties, even early seventies—play in encouraging their parents to "just begin" a program of fitness, and to "stay the course" during the early days of trying it out. As such, I wrote this Super-Senior Health Guide to encourage many more adult children of super-seniors to get their parents started in a similar at-home program, or to persuade caregivers and therapists to implement this program in their facilities.

Read this book; then share it with your super-senior parents or elderly relatives and friends. As noted earlier, there are some twenty million super-seniors over 75. That number is going to increase to forty million in less than thirty years. There's going to be a massive emphasis in future decades on keeping super-seniors (who are tending to live even longer lives) healthier. Your concern should not only be this, but also to help them live these longer lives better, happier.

Remember, too, that the success of a full-spectrum health regimen depends on the ease that most ultra-seniors can participate in all the parameters of a program involving physical exercise, sound nutrition, interaction with others, personal interests, hygiene, and mobility. *Wellness For Super-Seniors* provides the tools to do so while encapsulating the essence of the term "ease of action" into the entire regimen.

For example, Juan's Total Wellness for Over-75's fitness program offers an exercise routine that *any senior aged 75 to 100* can do and enjoy doing so!

The exercises are not only relatively easy; they are not

uncomfortable, nor painful. The adage, "no pain, no gain," does not apply here. And yet there *is* gain! My specially designed exercises actually help to shape and develop strength in the upper body (arms, shoulders, chest) and core (especially the lower back), with maximum concentration on legs and posture (to dramatically improve balance, which is a crucial concern of all seniors).

A Better Roadmap

You need a clear roadmap of what to do for super-seniors during those potential medical-onset years. Sure you worry. Your time and energy may be called upon more and more, diverted from what you otherwise would like to do, to seeing to the needs of your parent.

If you find yourself increasingly concerned about your parent's flexibility, health or balance, you are far from being unique. Millions of boomers and young-seniors are coping with the same concerns as you are. All are worried about the fitness and mobility of older loved ones because you *do* love them.

You don't want to see your parent/s fall.

You don't want to see them bedridden with osteoporosis or contract diabetes. You especially don't want a parent to have a stroke. You know that if one of your parents goes to hospital or a nursing home—say, as a result of a fall resulting in a fractured hip—he may get further complications (pneumonia, C-Diff, MRSA, depression, infection) while undergoing recovery from surgery, rehabilitation and/or physical therapy.

Here's how I inadvertently helped develop a new lifestyle roadmap for someone I cared for—not a parent, but a very close friend—and in so doing, developed a game plan for others. It's an example of how SSHG turns despondence and lethargy into renewed interest and vibrancy.

I developed a close relationship with an 87-year-old nearly a decade ago. We were both active on the finance council of a local organization. Frank was with the U.S. Army during the Second World War: his personal heroism and command story in the European theatre after D-Day ranks every bit as fascinating as any of those recounted in Tom Brokaw's book *The Greatest Generation*. Two years on, Frank had an ugly fall while leaving church on a windy Sunday. After a stay in the hospital to mend his broken shoulder—plus further time in a rehab nursing facility—he returned home using a walker. He seemed to be a changed man, his level of self-confidence and usual exuberance at low ebb.

That proved to be a turning point for both of us. I offered to coach Frank at home in the special exercises I had developed for myself some years earlier—a story I'll touch on later. The exercises consisted of standing or seated isometrics, involving no equipment or weights, along with a warm up routine of easy stretches and a closing period of mild aerobics. I blended in the occasional discussion on healthy eating and common-sense nutritional habits that I was, at the time, still refining and writing about. We would jointly peruse articles and medical newsletters—from clinics and medical centers such as Mayo, Harvard, Princeton, Pritikin, Cleveland and Johns Hopkins—touching on certain health issues, wellness strategies, and the so-called "diseases-of-affluence."

Frank became so enthusiastic about my program, he insisted that all the parameters (exercise, nutrition, medical awareness) should be taught to many more seniors his age and even those much younger. His exuberance returned, and his zest for living shone again—so much so that we sometimes played nine holes of golf, we ate out once or twice a week, and we started a local group class. Frank accompanied me as I met with directors of community centers and retirement complexes, and as I prepared for radio interviews and a live cooking and exercise class demonstration for an ABC affiliate television station in Hartford, Connecticut. We did indeed start several regular "Juan's Total Wellness for Over-75s" classes at venues in Rhode Island and Connecticut, with average attendance of ten or twelve super-seniors per session.

Frank became a regular "student," a constant attendee, as well as an advocate for my classes from the beginning. He would say that he could not have done it if the entire program had not: 1) been "readily doable," 2) been a joy to participate in, and 3) been easy to accomplish the modest goals set.

In those early years, Frank lost some weight and took in two notches on his belt. He looked stronger and walked taller. He had some further setbacks over the next eight years, to be sure, but was able to recover without undue loss of confidence, without depression or deep anxiety. Frank always had the enthusiastic support of his son and daughter and their families, visits from grandchildren, and constant contact with close friends and former college students of his. At the same time, he was an inspiration to his newfound exercise classmates, cracking jokes and encouraging them to try harder.

Frank's is just one story—albeit an important one—illustrating the impact of interaction and persuasion of younger persons (family and friends) on health. His story shows the mutual enjoyment and vitality developed by his living longer well.

Note on Health and Safety

What you younger encouragers and facilitators come to realize during this process is that you, too, will be super-seniors one day— usually sooner than expected—and some other younger person will probably be looking after you and seeing to your wellbeing. That is exactly what I found out six or seven years ago with Frank. The time to anticipate adopting a total wellness regimen is *now*, not later. Losing a bit of weight at 55 is far easier than trying to do so ten or twenty years down the road . . . indeed it can become diabolically hard to do so at 75 years of age. Excess weight is not good for hips and knees—possibly a catalyst for subsequent knee and/or hip replacement. Being overweight or obese can affect posture, gait, and balance. The associated difficulties can snowball—lethargy, propensity to fall, cessation of walking and gardening, and further inactivity leading to serious medical issues.

You will find that most people in the mid-eighties and above are rarely *completely* healthy. Men and women in the super-seniors' group who are at that age will likely have at least one chronic medical condition. Almost all will be on some form of daily prescription medication; and a certain percentage will fall into a "less-active" or "more-frail" or "non-ambulatory" category.

What this group needs—although certainly not all—are the tools to help them *maintain function*. They—and even some of their somewhat younger super-seniors who may also fall into the "more-frail" or "dementia" categories—need a continuing lifestyle regimen to allow, to the greatest extent possible, independent functioning in activities of daily living, such as dressing, bathing, toileting, eating, getting up, walking, basic housekeeping, and some level of discourse.

The objectives of a "maintain function" program should seek to deal not solely with the physical aspects of health—such as promoted in "Juan's Total Wellness for Over-75s" exercises and nutrition sections—but should include aspects of mental and psychological health: that is, enhancing the ability to communicate, the desire to socialize, being able to sleep satisfactorily, and to spur ambition in caring for oneself through adequate nutrition and hygiene.

The issue of safety is obviously a major concern for super-seniors. The fear of falling and hurting oneself—which can be followed by getting very sick, either in hospital or at home—preys on the mental and psychological health of all elderly people. Physical condition, a level of fitness gained through moderate exercise, helps to counteract that fear and reduce the risk of a serious fall. It's an elder-life lesson that illustrates the need for improved balance, strength, and posture.

The Three Pillars

The three pillars, or basic toolbox, of "Juan's Total Wellness for Over-75s" program comprise: (1) Juan's special Exercises; (2) healthful Nutrition; and (3) Awareness of certain, "potentially-avoidable" medical conditions.

The three-pillar regimen will address many of the issues discussed above and, in conjunction with good medical care, can be considered essential for maintaining and maximizing—for the very elderly—their functioning and well being. Of course, as you now know, the *optimum* time to start or re-start a total wellness regimen, and to adopt an adjusted lifestyle, is not as a very elderly super-senior but as early in mid-life (or just-retired life) as possible. However, any time is a good time.

Recapping Key Questions

So, let me ask you the question then: who is primarily concerned about your parents' wellbeing and health as they transition from the seventies to the eighties? Is it you? Or is it them? Do they care? Perhaps it's a healthier spouse—say, a partner of one who may have dementia or another complication?

You, as responsible children, are concerned not only for the well being of your aging parents—whom you love—but for your own and your family's peace of mind. You are motivated to ensure, as best you can, that there is not an early repeat of an intestinal problem; not another heart attack; not another mini-stroke; not another car accident; not another inexplicably-adverse reaction from a new prescription medication; not another nighttime fall in the bathroom.

Becoming more and more involved in your parents' wellbeing, you gradually become more acutely aware of your own—and your husband's—"health condition." You ask: "What about *my* own health?" You may be uncomfortable, even worried or depressed *if* you have been idle and lethargic for the past couple of decades. I was in that very situation twenty-five years ago. You may be over-weight; your endurance may be so poor that if you climb a flight of stairs you are winded or exhausted; you may be reluctant to walk or perform mild exercise; you may be overeating—especially the wrong foods and drinks such as over-stuffed white bread sandwiches, french-fries, salted snacks, foods saturated with bad fats, breakfast pastries, heavy deserts, sugared drinks, excess alcohol, 14-ounce steaks; and fall entirely short on large green salads, multiple vegetables, fresh fruits, omega-3-loaded (wild-caught) fish, and whole grains.

If you are a little worried, then those who will care for you, or see to your care, i.e. your own children—for they will eventually look after you as you grow much older—will become even more concerned. In addition to the emotional strain of seeing to the care of much-loved aging parents, the financial burdens (both on a national scale and at a personal level) associated with geriatric health care in the decades ahead will become incredibly alarming to younger generations, perhaps intolerable.

Wellness For Super-Seniors—in setting out certain essential tools for revitalization of our present super-seniors—will involve modification of their lifestyle/s. And, as their child, yours too! But rest assured: adjusting their, and your, lifestyle is not that difficult once begun. Understanding and following the guidance and regimen pertaining to "Juan's Total Wellness for Over-75s" three pillars will involve you in sheer exhilaration and bring you back to that feeling of fitness and joie de vivre you may have had twenty or thirty years earlier. The hardest part is just starting. *Of course* it is difficult to change the habits of a quarter of a century. But you can, and you will. I know, because I have been through it all and seen hundreds of others do so as well.

How Do I Know?

I'm in my eightieth year; less than a year away from that birthday that some call "the mighty eighty." The eighties and nineties can be wonderful years! I play a little golf, write a bit, paint often, and read voraciously. I travel internationally, sometimes on business, mostly for pleasure. I'm called a "community organizer" because I initiate and conduct fitness classes for super- and ultra-seniors. I exercise— still run (but not full marathons)—and hope to continue doing so for years to come. I am merely one of many: the rapidly expanding group of 75 to 100s who are now living so much longer. I am working to make those additional years BETTER years, for all of us—the very old, and the not-so-very-old.

This is what led me to develop my own revised total health regimen: I am most fortunate, for I should have died—like my father and all his male siblings—before the age of 55. Not only did I have some of the same genes, I was forty pounds overweight, traveled constantly and continually under pressure, ate atrociously, never exercised, drank too much, and smoked: a death sentence routine.

When younger, in my early fifties, I did not take advice on how to live healthily during the approaching mid-sixties or post-retirement years. As a professional researcher I should have been able to foresee the future in that regard. I spent decades directing statistical studies and analyzing data, resolving corporate strategies based on facts and trends.

On retiring early, I found myself with a similar challenge in a very different milieu. Through two wrenching personal experiences, a rehabilitation period, then extensive research in this new field, I began to analyze the constantly evolving data and information relating to ailments and lifestyle-problems affecting the aging. Even before that period of learning, I had been led, through the influence of a business acquaintance, to dramatically change my own living habits.

In time, my new lifestyle, coupled to further reading and research and the encouragement of friends and former military peers, convinced me to articulate and refine a comprehensive "total wellness game plan" so that others—young and old—would not find themselves without a roadmap for a better life in *their* early retirement years and the later super- and ultra-seniors years.

Living "BETTER" during those extra twenty-five years from 75 to 100 involves significant lifestyle adjustments:

- Physical fitness through exercise
- Consumption of more nutritious foods
- Being aware of, and understand, aspects of potentially avoidable diseases
- Maintaining a positive outlook and young-at-heart attitude.

From a "sound nutrition" standpoint, once I understood the true merits of "good foods" and the dangers of "bad fats, sugars, salt," and so on, I had little trouble in adapting my own recipes and meal servings. For the prior forty years, I had been a home chef, preparing most meals and experimenting with cookbooks brought back from around the world. I also learned nutrition principles, particularly as they affect health, from attendance at the renowned Pritikin Longevity Center. My wife and I first went to Pritikin for two full weeks twenty-three years ago. That visit changed, and may certainly have saved, my life. Since then I have returned to Pritikin on several occasions.

The nutrition and diet adjustment was the easier part. The physical fitness angle provided more of a challenge. I came to understand the delicate situation of some of my students as I worked with them. One day, early on in the process, I arrived at the auditorium where my group was assembling near their chairs. As I greeted them, one dear lady who had her back to me tried to look over her shoulder—instead of turning slowly around—and proceeded to fall toward me. I stepped forward quickly and caught her in my arms, but her weight and momentum by that time were too much for my strength, and we both tumbled backwards on the carpeted floor. I wound up lying underneath, she on top of me, and she looked me in the eye and asked, "are *you* alright?" No harm was done, but it was one more lesson for me in realizing that exercises and lecture routines for super-seniors had to be different from those conducted in classes for younger folk.

Developing a set of beneficial exercises that could be readily conducted by individuals as "young" as the mid-seventies, as well as by those in their eighties and 90s—some participants would undoubtedly also be using walkers or accompanied by personal caregivers, a few even in wheelchairs—was what I had to solve. And I did.

The 50 isometric, stretch, and simple aerobic exercises presented in this manual have been tried and tested over several years, in group and individual classes involving people ranging in ages from 72 to 98.

The exercises:

- Harden and tone important muscles
- Improve balance and leg strength
- Correct posture

In the classes themselves, an added bonus is that the program fosters an astonishingly warm camaraderie between participants. Those in their seventies find they are standing beside—and sometimes steadying—the late-eighty and ninety-year-olds. And they benefit greatly from doing so. The same camaraderie and bonding will take place between you "youngsters" in the your fifties and sixties, and your parents. You may find that you will be coaching and working with your parents in building and maintaining their *"better"* elder years, or standing beside them as they work with another caregiver or therapist.

I can now document my total wellness regimen as a certified personal fitness trainer and proven instructor specializing in that population group of over-75's super-seniors. I re-learned, studied, and trained with health and fitness organizations: NCSF (National

Council on Strength & Fitness), AFAA (Aerobics & Fitness Association of America), and immersion weeks at Pritikin Longevity Center several times over the past two decades. I bring my expertise with confidence into both large fitness classes and one-on-one health seminars.

This is a lifestyle game plan, designed and developed specifically for our super-senior age groups, which may be adopted by you, their offspring. When you get to be eighty or eighty-five, you will be very different from your grandparents—and perhaps from your own parents—in that you will have started far earlier to prepare for that penultimate decade.

That decade, and subsequently when you are in your nineties, will be far better for the very old. This book can change many, many of your lives.

Chapter 2.

Is This Super-Senior Health Guide For You?

Our Future Together

In certain cultures, especially in bygone eras—in the Far East, in Latin America, in North America (with our Native Americans)—the very old were given respect, were listened to, were touched and held. They taught younger generations the lessons of the soul and secrets to resiliency and wisdom. In the United States today, and in much of Europe, we are in danger of ignoring the needs of the very old rather than embracing and harnessing their unique life experiences, knowledge, and contribution to society.

We have to make greater efforts to reduce the risk of such a misinformed mistake, especially as our older population groups— those over-75's in America—will double in number, from 20 to 40 million within two decades.

Think about your own future in your eighties and nineties. Can you imagine heated conversations in 2033—more intense, by far, than those today—between segments of younger population groups, including officials and representatives in government as how best to deal with the potentially enormous costs of caring for the health of the long-lived very old? Those conversations may foster antipathy toward you as you age, not respect, warmth, or love. And those conversations may gravitate to a more bitter debate by 2055 as the number of 75's to 100 escalates to over 60 million citizens.

The work you do to help your elderly parent/s today can lead to a better future: to shape better years for those 75's to 100-year-olds; and to promote to "the younger set," your children, that the very old be lovingly nurtured and encouraged by them.

This is why I am so passionate in my mission: to help more super-seniors practice the "total wellness" principles set out herein; and to keep on urging that they *deserve* to receive extra-special and continual attention from their children, friends, young volunteers, caregivers, and in a different but vitally important context, from legislators, policy makers and representatives in government.

This is for *our* future together.

Why The Three Pillars

As noted in the preceding pages, the instruments in "Juan's Total Wellness Program for Over-75's" (what I call the toolbox), are compartmentalized into three overarching disciplines.

The first pillar is **Physical Fitness**—comprising anaerobic exercises for strengthening, balance, and posture; and moderate aerobic exercises for circulation, movement, and stretching.

The second discipline is **Sound Nutrition**—involving sensible eating habits (without fasting or extreme diets) that protect the heart, reduce plaque in the arteries, lower LDL cholesterol, minimize caloric intake yet totally satisfy hunger.

The third pillar is **Health Awareness**—a primer in imparting, in layman's language but primarily through lectures given by medical professionals, fundamental knowledge about the so-called "diseases of affluence" (which I designate as "mostly-avoidable" diseases) that have afflicted Americans and Europeans at an accelerating pace over the past eighty years; and how to cope with—i.e. lessen and even reverse—their deleterious impact on super-seniors' lives.

There *are* certain men and women in their eighties who still (incredibly) run marathons and other races, who prefer to walk a full eighteen holes when playing golf, who swim a mile each day. Some even do triathlons. A few perform strenuous anaerobic gym exercises with weights and machines. But they are the exceptions. And they are, indeed, exceptional!

Most seniors, however, in their late-seventies, eighties, and nineties are not able, nor do they want, to get into difficult positions on a gym floor, or workout with complex weight-bearing machines. In regard to aerobic exercise, many of our ultra-seniors, who worry about balance and the risk of falling, do not care to stride on a treadmill or step up to rotating elliptical pedals.

And yet, these same super- and ultra-seniors well through their nineties can, and do benefit from a regular regimen of non-threatening and enjoyable anaerobic activity, coupled to gradually re-learning postural confidence and "walking tall."

Exercise alone, however, is not enough. For many super-seniors—indeed for all age brackets—nutrition is equally important as regular exercise in warding off the creeping onset of one or more of those mostly-avoidable "diseases of affluence." Lastly, the third pillar—comprising health and medical issues' awareness—serves not only to educate in lay terms the causes of many of those late-in-life maladies, but also to reinforce your motivation to undertake the entire total wellness regimen.

That's precisely the goal of "Juan's Total Wellness for Over-75's" program. It is to instill confidence through improved strength and balance to the two oldest population groups. It is to instruct seniors, who may have become sedentary or overweight, to be aware of the joy of revitalization through deep breathing, erect posture, toned muscles, and sensible, healthful eating habits.

This next assertion is very important and I don't hesitate to repeat it over and over in my Super-Senior Health Guide: "Juan's Total Wellness for Over 75's" anaerobic exercises *can be performed* by otherwise sedentary men and women; those who are bent over and who use walkers; those who are recovering from serious falls; any who may have sustained fractures or breaks as well as those, in particular, who's confidence may have been temporarily shattered.

Do not be afraid.

The fundamental purpose of this game plan is to restructure the living habits and lifestyles of men and women in their mid-seventies and beyond who have become relatively inactive, so that they feel a hundred percent healthier, happier, rejuvenated, and prepared to not only live far longer but "to live longer, *better*!"

Better . . . that's the new key word, the essential condition to living so much longer unburdened by excessive worry or fear.

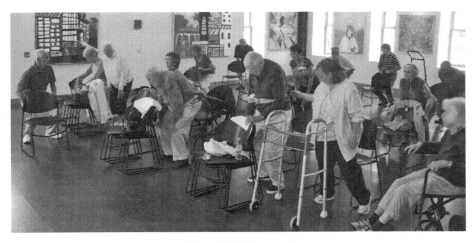

Juan's Wellness class

Chapter 3.

True Transitions, Convincing Life Lessons

Learning From Others

You'll find in the following two stories reasons why I believe you shouldn't hesitate to make a recommendation to someone else who you think may benefit enormously (whether a super-senior or a person your age or younger) by making a dramatic change to his or her lifestyle; and why it's so important to nurture, care for, and encourage the very old—vis-à-vis health and quality of life— especially your own parents . . . for their sake, and as a bonus to reap a surprisingly joyful experience yourself.

Younger seniors, especially you who are just at or approaching normal retirement age, can learn a lot from others: those who have undergone problems associated with early diseases or poor living habits; those who have themselves transitioned through a beneficial change in lifestyle; those who have dealt with difficulties that sometimes arise in arranging for the care of an elderly parent or relative.

I was the fortunate recipient of such advice.

We younger seniors, you and I who are anywhere from fifty to eighty years of age, can take a voluntary role assisting in the care and nurturing of an ultra-senior ("ultra-seniors" are those I categorize in the age group of 85 and over). Of the millions in this ultra group— over nine million today (increasing to 20 million by 2030)—many do not have anyone to visit them, talk to them, or take an interest in them. Some ultra-seniors are of course visited by a relative from time to time, while they languish in a nursing home or dementia unit. Many are yearning for so much more. Those of you who give of your time, care, and nurturing in this regard, are as equally rewarded as those who receive; of this I am certain—I see it all the time.

My Story: Barely Alive at 55

Fitness was not part of my resume. Nor was nutrition and health awareness a priority in my life. I kept myself busy with a career. Developing this wellness program was a gradual process that began with saving my own life.

My father and all his brothers died in their mid-fifties of heart attacks. They all smoked. Though not obese or overweight, none were athletic. They were sedentary with type A personalities.

At 55, I duplicated the general male story of my father's family. Overweight by one third of my ideal weight, I weighed 185 pounds on a 140-pound frame. I traveled to all parts of the world, away from home three-quarters of the time, smoked a pack of cigarettes a day, ate poorly, and drank too much. In addition to the physical negatives, I undoubtedly became over-stressed.

During a business luncheon with an executive of a commercial airline company, my client and friend eventually paused and said: "Juan, you don't look well. Can I be frank with you?" He continued by telling me about his own experience. Having suffered a mild heart attack some eight months earlier, he went, at his cardiologist's recommendation, to a unique wellness clinic called Pritikin Longevity Center. After three weeks of a monitored regimen involving exercises and a strict low-fat, low-calorie nutritional eating plan, coupled to daily medical lectures from the six attending physicians on America's "diseases of affluence" and alternative health-promoting habits, his total cholesterol dropped thirty-five percent; his blood pressure became normal; and he stopped being stressed most of the time.

"Take a couple weeks off. Go to the Pritikin Longevity Center in Santa Monica, or the one in Florida. You'll get a full physical before you start the program. Take your wife with you. I know that for me," my friend reiterated, "it was a seismic wake-up call. It completely changed my life. It may have saved my life."

This kindly and concerned man related additional aspects of his new lifestyle and discussed the priorities one should consider in the context of business, personal, and family matters. I listened to him and thought deeply (as I toyed with a tuna-melt while he finished his large green salad).

That very weekend, before commuting back to my overseas corporate head office, I stopped at my home in Connecticut and spoke with my wife. With her agreement, I made a reservation for both of us at Pritikin for the following month, for a two-week stay. Then I traveled to the group headquarters and had another conversation with my chairman.

I took my airline friend's advice. Indeed, I went further. In essence I pulled the eject handle and bailed out of one lifestyle to chart a ride in a different direction. I set an alternate flight path.

My wife accompanied me to Pritikin Longevity Center for a two-week stay. The regimen at Pritikin in California reduced my total cholesterol to an astonishingly low level. My wife's dropped even more, in percentage terms. The Pritikin experience "kick-started" us into maintaining an entirely revised plan of nutritious-eating and moderate exercise.

Back home, I started running in the early mornings with a neighbor. In the first few weeks, I became exhausted quickly, and I would stop and walk after only half a mile of running at his speed. That changed. Within a few months I kept up with my neighbor, running three or four miles at a decent pace. My weight continued to drop. I felt wonderful, revitalized—like a new human being.

The following year I went into long-distance running training and registered for the Marine Corps Marathon in Washington, D.C.

It is called "the beginner's marathon," and so it was. It was the year after Oprah ran the Marine Corps Marathon and her accomplishment inspired me into thinking I could train and run a marathon, too. I managed to finish, but it was tough. I trained harder after that, and ran several more marathons and a number of long-distance races over the ensuing years.

In 2006, at age 73, I went to a fiftieth-year reunion of my U.S. Marine Corps officers' Basic School class. I felt more like 43 as I went out for morning runs along the San Diego harbor-front. That final evening, at the main banquet on the venerable aircraft carrier USS Midway, some of my former squadron friends asked, intrigued: "Juan (or Irish, as I was known), what are you doing to look so good?"

I outlined for my peers what I was doing. I explained my new regimen, covering aspects of diet and nutrition, exercise, and awareness of certain diseases, especially as those issues affect the aging process. During the following few weeks, after answering additional email queries from old Marine friends, I gradually came to realize that I could help others in my age group and older to become healthier.

I expanded the series of special isometric exercises I had developed so that even super- and ultra-seniors in their 80's and 90's could perform them (without having to get down on the floor, or travel to a gym, or resort to using weights or equipment), and I added an easy set of light aerobic exercises.

I studied and took courses from NCSF (National Council on Strength and Fitness) and AFAA (Aerobics and Fitness Association of America), and completed additional courses and the exam to become a Certified Personal Fitness Trainer, possibly one of the oldest at that time.

I printed documents and newsletters, set up a business with a website, and—as touched on earlier, with my friend Frank's encouragement—began classes for over-75's. I gave several radio interviews and a television demonstration, speaking to the importance of both exercise and nutrition—NOT just one or the other. At the conclusion of every interview, the interviewer's parting comments would invariably include something like: "*I wish my father* (or my mother) *could do this program*"; or, "this should all be in a book."

I share my story because I feel that if I could choose this new lifestyle and stay with it, it may help to persuade you and your parents to do so, too.

However, it is not always easy, either to change oneself or to look after and nurture some of the very old. A percentage of super-seniors are blessed with great genes and have lived relatively active and healthy lives, and they are a joy to look after and participate in their later-years' care. But many are not so blessed; and many super- and ultra-seniors do not have a close loved one to care for them, or help them in their long-term care planning and in the conduct of their personal affairs.

The second story (below) is one of a potentially difficult case, illustrating a need—in certain instances—for reaching out to a non-relative or a distant relative who may have great need of help. There are wolves lurking to prey on the very old, a situation that could get worse as the population groups of super-seniors double in the decades ahead.

Geraldine's Story: Nurturing a Losing Life

I was awakened to the adverse circumstances surrounding the health, financial, and emotional issues of those who are old and alone through interaction with an elderly relative. I became her primary caregiver.

It's not always easy being a caregiver. It can involve being guardian, companion, power-of-attorney, accountant, medical matters' arranger, constant visitor, defender, and more. I took Geraldine—my 78-year-old first cousin (who is now 89)—from an isolated, unhealthy, "taken-advantage-of" existence and, over time, gave her back her dignity and arranged for the assisted care she rightly deserved.

Rescuing Gerry didn't merely involve getting her out of a difficult financial and unsustainable living situation; it meant redirecting her entire lifestyle, re-instilling purpose to her living, and devising a wellness strategy for her next fifteen or more years.

Geraldine's sister Sarah died in early 2002. The two reclusive sisters, then 78 and 77, had lived together all their lives. During careers in advertising and publishing in New York City, they shared an apartment near Park Avenue, not far from Grand Central Station. They were icons of fashion, regularly attending the Met, away on weekend tours to the country, and occasionally traveled to Europe's capitals.

After retirement in the 1980's, the sisters relocated to Texas to what they thought would be a lower cost environment. Sarah became quite ill during the last two years of her life, and by early 2001 she became bedridden. She retained the part-time assistance of a home-care attendant through a firm that provided such services. Gerry was not well herself and, at times, was somewhat confused, in no position to look after Sarah, or to monitor and control the home-care attendant's hours or performance. What started as affordable assistance in early 2001 escalated to three-thousand-dollar-a-week full-time "service" by year-end. They were being taken advantage of and financially abused. I made the first of several trips from Connecticut to Texas to help Gerry.

The last two weeks of Sarah's life were in a hospital ICU. No independent home care attendants were allowed into the ICU; yet the agency billed the sisters for "twenty-four-seven" care service during those final weeks. That, I was told by a local attorney, was a not uncommon example of how the very elderly and the sick, those who do not have counsel and help, may become rapidly impoverished.

The National Center on Elder Abuse reported in 2010 (based on a U.S. Senate Special Committee on Aging finding) that some five million seniors are victims of "elder abuse" each year—most of it related to financial matters.

Gerry inherited Sarah's estate, which included an IRA and some additional investments. I realized the combined portfolios of the two sisters could provide Gerry with sufficient income, if managed prudently, to live out a long life in relative comfort.

Within three weeks of Sarah's death, Gerry had a serious fall in her apartment. I returned to Texas: my fifth trip in two months. Gerry was in the same hospital with a fractured hip and a broken shoulder. She developed pneumonia and was transferred to the ICU. During the time she was in ICU (for nearly two weeks) the former caregiver, or a partner, sat in the hospital waiting room. When I reviewed statements from the agency, I found they were billing for twenty-four-hours-a-day attendance, even for non-existent night shifts.

The caregiver, by now, had taken full control. She had access to Gerry's apartment, keys, purse, mail, and checkbook. She filled out and signed checks for selected billings—duplicating Gerry's signature—including weekly invoices from the home care agency itself.

I discharged the home care attendant in the hospital, causing consternation in the quiet corridors. I called the owner/manager of the home care agency to say I would be following up legally, and that we would not pay certain major portions of their remaining weekly billings.

The Texas lawyer I retained said that the incidence of single, elderly people being taken advantage of in a similar manner was far more frequent than one might imagine. Gerry's life savings (including the inherited funds of Sarah's estate) could have been wholly absorbed—if not by the home care agency, then by the individual "caregivers"—within two or three years.

During Gerry's subsequent stay in a rehab nursing home, the professionals there concluded that she would have to use a walker on a permanent basis and, given her ancillary ailments, she would need assisted living care at a minimum. I determined it would be best for her to return to Connecticut and be near me, to which Gerry agreed. Over the next month I made all the necessary arrangements.

Gerry's prescription medications escalated from five to eight—drugs for anxiety, depression, hypertension, osteoporosis, thyroid, heart, bladder, and irritable bowel syndrome—plus an assortment of over-the-counter pills.

We found Gerry a two-room unit in a nearby assisted living home, and we took care of administering her medications on a daily basis.

After seven years of encouragement and coercion, coaxing and nurturing, Gerry's health took a downturn. During a stay in hospital, she contracted pneumonia and one of the gut infections that frequent some nursing homes and hospitals. After a period of time in ICU she was transferred to a rehab center in the vicinity of the hospital, ostensibly to prepare her to return to her assisted living facility rooms.

The manner in which Gerry's nurses and therapists handled her for 28 days bordered on incompetence. Geraldine's prescription ordered her to undergo physical therapy twice a day. She actually attended seated physical therapy sessions with a group of several other patients an estimated 25 times total, if that. When the facility's invoices (that I obtained copies of) were submitted to Medicare, Geraldine was charged for 76 physical therapy sessions during her 28 days in rehab—more than twice a day—with simultaneous billing for 76 periods of "occupational therapy" and billings for 35 simultaneous periods of "speech pathology."

Total "therapy" billings to Medicare for Gerry, as a virtually bedridden patient, for what should have been about 25 physical therapy sessions costing $1,600, turned into 187 "therapy & pathology" joint sessions, for a total of $14,000—nine times the probable justifiable amount.

Gerry deteriorated rapidly. The rehab center recommended that Gerry not be permitted to return to her assisted living home "because," the director said, "she's incontinent, demented, and incapable of walking." I discharged Gerry within the hour, dressed her, and slowly but surely *walked* her out of that facility. She thanked all the staff as we departed.

My family and I took Gerry home, fed her three or four small meals a day, walked her, exercised her, cleaned her, and talked with her often. Over a period of four weeks we brought her back to life, put a few pounds on her 90-pound frame, made her smile and read again, and convinced her that she could walk alone (with a walker) and dress herself. Gerry told me stories of my father that I had never heard before. She made us all laugh with her tales of Madison Avenue executives, work deadlines, and mild scandals during her sister's and her New York careers. She started enjoying *living* once again.

The nine-year learning curve with Gerry was monumental. I had no initial inkling what the very-elderly might have to go through, not only if they were alone and destitute, but even if they had the solicitous attendance of a family member, well-meaning but unversed. Complete caring involves not only the physical aspect of a certain element of fitness, not only sound nutrition, not only regular visits to physicians and clinics, but the loving, constant personal interaction of someone close or who really cares. The experience in looking after Geraldine imparted a much-needed education on the *real* meaning of caring and wellness for those who are alone and lonely, especially during those super-senior years, the potentially wonderful ages comprising the 80's and 90's.

Juan and Gerry

Chapter 4.

Implementing A New Lifestyle

Pillar I: Fitness And Exercise

The Logic

Over the past five years, I initiated classes at different locations and gradually honed the exercise-nutrition syllabus into comfortable, one-hour sessions. I conducted the classes a set number of times a week (two or three), in course rotations entailing three months' duration. The one-hour format allowed some time within each exercise period to talk about—or to distribute a handout dealing with—the subject of nutrition, food selection, label reading, caloric density, meal preparation, and menus/recipes.

The three-month course rotation schedule also allowed at least one class for a guest lecturer—a visiting physician—to address an aspect of health awareness, i.e. a medical research study, a specific set of diseases and prevention methods, and/or medically-approved lifestyle recommendation/s.

The attendees to my early classes—"students," I affectionately call them—numbered between ten and twelve, a manageable size group to be able to teach and at the same time carefully monitor. Each one-hour class comprised roughly fifty minutes of exercises, and ten minutes' discussion on a nutrition or health subject. Handouts, if distributed, comprised my quarterly newsletters, professional medical health-letters (e.g. from Mayo, Harvard, Pritikin, Princeton, Cleveland, Johns Hopkins and other clinics and institutions), health or nutrition news articles, and homework assignments.

Many people seek out exercise programs solely to lose weight, some impatient to see and feel immediate results. My wellness regimen does not meet that latter goal: that's unhealthy, anyway. For those who are overweight and have a clear and realistic target of losing a certain percent of their excess body mass, my total wellness program—when followed diligently—will help them lose weight over a period of several months while restoring strength and reforming muscle.

A few years ago, after the second class of a new, bi-monthly rotation, a group of three younger ladies (*under*-75's) approached and asked, "Is that all there is?" I answered affirmatively, and explained that with my "self-elasto" isometric exercises, the benefits and awareness of renewed strength, upper-body firmness, posture, and balance, improvement becomes evident after several weeks—depending on the level of effort exerted. For that group of ladies,

"Juan's Total Wellness for Over-75's"—at least the exercise sector—was not enough.

I understand when some people who are already fit and strong prefer to have a more strenuous physical challenge. They need to work out in a gym or spa environment with aerobic equipment, machines, and weights. However, for most of my super- and ultra-senior students who stay the course for a three-month rotation, the physical change is noticeable, and almost all stay on for additional rotations. At least two-thirds of my students have been class attendees for two years or more.

Heartwarming Reactions

Unsolicited written and verbal comments and year-end assessments from past and present students bear out the merits of the "total wellness" aspects of this program, and the results of their own efforts. One gentleman (aged 76; I'll call him Phillip) attended my classes for over a year, then elected to transfer to a local gym to begin lifting weights and use a treadmill for increased aerobic activity. He felt he could now do so, whereas a year and a half earlier, when he started my program, he was plagued with arthritis in his knees and problems from a right hip replacement. He also had atrial fibrillation and, even though a tall man, was overweight at 240 pounds. At the end of his first year, after he lost forty pounds, lowering his BMI to "somewhat overweight" instead of the formerly "seriously overweight" level, he wrote a personal assessment of my program:

"Juan, you'd suggested at the outset that I might find the exercises pretty 'gentle'—and I did—but I also found that they offered just the level of activity I needed to get started again after years of inactivity. In fact, now that I'm familiar with them and how they should feel, I can turn up the heat at will, stretching further, pressing harder . . . and getting an increasing benefit with each successive class. What could be better next time? Not much. There's a nice blend of useful nutritional information that serves as an ongoing reminder to be more conscious of what we eat. I've been inspired to continue a daily regimen of calorie control, targeting another 20-lb. weight loss over the next two nine-week rotations. As to the exercise routine, the repetitive aspect is a good thing. It allows the 'comfort' of a familiar and predictable routine in each session. Having said that, I had been impressed in reading that you had developed some fifty exercises for super-seniors . . . you might want to introduce one additional variation each week. Regarding the nutrition advice, I like your approach, a sprinkling of suggestions throughout; just enough to permit a rethinking of eating habits for those wanting to lose weight or in eating healthier foods. Finally, considering the health awareness segments, it probably can't be overdone. It is a good chance to adopt health awareness as a natural mindset. You certainly make it inviting for those who haven't given it much thought, or who may have tried and given up pursuing it. You provide an excellent role model in your own physique, energy and demeanor; and in keeping us from being self-conscious by your own sincere execution of every exercise with us, each seemingly as fresh and focused as the first time you ever did it. It makes for an engaging and worthwhile hour."

A 94-year-old who has been with me for three years wrote a short critique at the start of his second year:

"I am convinced that your 'total wellness' program has made me stronger than I was a year ago. I tightened my belt by two notches; and I still need to take another two inches off my waist—and I will."

A very fit eighty-year-old (a regular summertime ocean swimmer) wrote:

"I was pleasantly surprised: the exercises are very useful and even for me a bit challenging. Since I am a 'back pain' candidate, I have to find ways to keep my back in shape in the winter; this program's exercises do that and I certainly will pursue them. As to nutrition, I did learn from this course to take seriously what to eat (not easy for a person who loves good bread, cheese, potatoes, and butter). I found the health awareness lectures and materials interesting and food for thought, especially in regard to high blood pressure."

An 80-year-old female student sent a postcard while away on a short vacation:

"I am in Virginia for a few days, but I'll practice my core exercises. Your fitness classes are wonderful. Can hardly believe how doing such painless routines can make me feel so good."

Another woman who had certain recurring medical complications said:

"When I started your program I felt tired and depressed much of the time; now I weigh 13 pounds less and I feel much stronger and so much better."

That sort of comment is typical for most of the women attendees. Not only do they feel good after their weekly or daily exercise routines, they begin to strengthen the muscles in their arms and thighs, noticeably firm-up upper torsos, and their balance improves from the extra concentration I place on multiple core and legs and lower back exercises—as well as the constant emphasis I place on posture, posture, posture!

"Juan's Total Wellness for Over-75's" is not a program of overnight miracles. It should take the better part of a three-month rotation of thrice-weekly anaerobic exercise periods to see a physical difference. The isometric exercises should be coupled to aerobic options such as marching-in-place or outdoor walking or treadmill activity along with adherence to Juan's Wellness nutrition guidelines, in order to lose weight (if needed to do so) and in order to notice the physical effects of stronger bodies, improved balance, better posture, reduced waistlines, and a new radiance from one's revitalized confidence.

The initial inkling of change will likely occur when other people notice the change in a super-senior. Your mother may hear comments, coupled to greetings, like: "oh, my dear, you are looking so well," or, "there's such a change in you; what are you doing?"

For those who really want, or need a much faster turnaround—such as after rehab following a fall or a post-op hospital stay, or to slough off seriously excessive weight in a hurry—it may be useful to consider having your parent kick-start a total wellness program with a concentrated, full-immersion, two- or three-week session. Dedicated periods of one to three weeks' duration, conducted with full-time supervision—either at home or at an equipped longevity center like Pritikin—can be extraordinarily beneficial. This is precisely what my wife and I did years ago when I decided to prolong my life and, to live to be older *better*.

Juan's class doing his isometric triceps strengthening exercises.

Chapter 5.

Celebrating The Game Plan

Pillar II: Nutrition And Diet

Satisfaction Guaranteed

Many of us-over-75's do not live in our own homes any more, particularly if we are mid-eighties and above. Some super-senior parents may have moved to retirement community complexes or to assisted living homes. They may have a choice of dining facilities for certain meals, with menu options as in a restaurant, or a dining room with set menus for all meals.

In such circumstances, your parents may do little or no cooking, and therefore it becomes harder to control the type of food they eat, the size of portions on their plate, and the levels of sugars, sodium, fats, and carbs in their daily diet.

Nevertheless, awareness of the *principles* of better nutrition can help them make wiser selections (if given options), or in the amounts of food groups served (if not given much choice); i.e. they can ask for a larger salad and for more fruit, they might leave half the meat, opt for whole wheat bread, insist on oatmeal in the morning, go easy on heavy cakes and cream-laden desserts.

For those super-senior parents still living in their own homes, shopping for food and preparing healthfully, simple yet delicious meals can be adventuresome and rewarding. Several of my "Juan's Total Wellness Program" class attendees in their 80's and 90's live in their own homes; in some cases their meals are provided by full-time caregivers, so it is often up to you as guardian to monitor or specify how they should be fed.

In my case, I live at home, and my wife and I both enjoy cooking and selecting wholesome foods. I have prepared meals for my family for most of the past fifty years. The rationale for including, in this book, a section on menus and recipes is a natural progression, since they are real examples that fit the guidelines given for healthy living, as part of "Juan's Total Wellness for Over-75's" program.

The essence of reasonable, sound nutrition is actually quite simple: consume much less fat; eat smaller portions of lean, white meat or fish protein; double the size of vegetable helpings and of your salads; minimize breads and beer; eat whole grains, brown rice and pastas; load up on legumes; consume lots of fruit; cut out salt; avoid sugary drinks and desserts.

The average American daily diet a decade and a half ago comprised 35% fat, 15% protein and 50% carbohydrate. Today, the average fat content is probably higher, nearer 40% caloric content. An added negative factor is that carbohydrates in the typical American diet are primarily refined flours and grain products, white rice, white pasta, white bread, etc.

In contrast, the nutritional balance advocated here (also closely matching Pritikin Longevity Center's) is 18% to 20% fat, 20% to 22% protein, and 58% to 60% carbohydrate. In regard to carbs, they should include vegetables and fruit rich in fiber and complex carbohydrates such as brown rice, brown breads, unrefined or unprocessed whole grains low in caloric density—in other words, they are filling without adding unwanted weight-inducing calories.

Similarly, the normal North American daily diet includes the equivalent of two teaspoons of sodium (salt) per day, infused as it is in all processed and canned or packaged foods (as well as from direct spreading over entrees) amounting to some 6,000 milligrams a day. The Pritikin nutrition regimen decreases salt levels to 1,000 or 1,200 milligrams a day, about one-fifth of the average American's intake. My "Juan's Total Wellness for Over-75's" nutrition guidelines result in average levels of about 1,500 milligrams a day, give or take.

The lowering of sodium intake, particularly in super-seniors approaching eighty or above, is important. Excess salt causes elevation in blood pressure, leading to hypertension (carrying few symptoms but with hidden associated risks). Probably the main reason people over eighty are admitted to emergency rooms is due to symptoms pointing to congestive heart failure, due to excess salt causing fluid to impact the lungs. When systolic blood pressure goes from normal to 160 or higher, the situation for over-80's may be classified as "dangerous" for risk of stroke. Other potential medical problems caused by excess sodium include damage to kidneys, and potential blockage of the vascular system. Salt is not the only culprit. Cardiologists advise that as we approach our 80's, we should not only minimize salt consumption but also learn to manage stress and anger, eliminate one or more prescription medication if possible, lose weight, cut down on alcohol consumption, and begin to exercise.

Sensible nutrition management, within a total wellness plan, is as vital as the element of physical exercise.

Combatting Causes

Proper nutrition is also important as a key factor inherent in the awareness, control, and avoidance of our first-world "diseases of affluence." They are nicknamed "diseases of affluence" because, in large part, they can be avoided through better-controlled lifestyle. Those maladies are prevalent in North America, primarily the United States, and they are the outcomes of an affluent, materially-pampered and/or overfed society.

The most common of these diseases are heart attack, stroke, heart failure, diabetes type 2, hypertension, premature dementia, osteoporosis, lung cancer, kidney disease, certain other cancers, and complications following a serious fall. The factors of affluence that bring about the potential for one or more of these maladies are: obesity, sedentary lifestyle, smoking, heavy alcoholic drinking, high LDL cholesterol from high-fat foods, high triglycerides from excessive sugars, high salt intake, high blood pressure, inability to control stress or anger, and total avoidance of natural, high-fiber healthy foods such as vegetables, salads, fruits, legumes, and whole grains.

For someone recovering from congestive heart failure symptoms, Pritikin Longevity Center might well advocate a balanced diet adding up to no more than 1,600 calories a day—along with carefully monitored and controlled exercise therapy. That diet could entail—as will be repeated so often, but in this case, more rigorously—very low sodium intake, no caffeine, minimal fats, no sugars, lots of dark-green leafy salads, multi-colored vegetables, fruits, oatmeal, whole wheat and whole grains, legumes, healthy desserts. My "Juan's Total Wellness for Over-75's" eating plan is more liberal than that particular Pritikin medical-recovery-regime, but still an extremely healthy diet.

For example, for a healthy, 5 foot 10 inch male weighing 160 pounds (with a BMI of 23/24) and already used to exercising several days a week, I would advocate a robust diet (but with the same principles discussed earlier) in sufficient quantity to add up to about 2,000-plus calories a day. The breakdown would be 400 calories from fat, 400 calories of protein, and 1,300 calories of carbs.

Regarding Weight Loss

Another example: for an individual wanting to lose substantial weight—to drop, say, from 190 to 165 pounds (lowering BMI from an "overweight" 28 to an "acceptable" 24 reading)—I would set a pragmatic time goal of six to eight months . . . on condition that (in addition to following my total wellness regimen of nutrition, exercise, health awareness) he or she would do twenty minutes of *aerobic* exercise four or five days a week.

There are some well-publicized superfast, "quick-loss," weight-reduction methods. It's not unusual to have read about one or another celebrity losing a huge amount of weight in a matter of weeks, not months. Such programs are often concentrated on high protein, high fiber regimens with meat, fowl, or fish prescribed three times a day, allowance of some legumes and limited vegetables but coupled to zero fruits, sugars, breads, rice, whole grains, starches, or potatoes. The caloric ratios in such programs are more like: fats 30 % to 40%; proteins 25% to 30%; carbs 35% to 40%. Fast and effective weight loss yes, but not necessarily the most nutritiously healthy—and not likely to be sustainable for the long term. What I would say is be careful, and be convinced it's best for you.

Some weight-loss or weight-control programs can also be quite costly. Some require personal coaching (on site, by phone or on-line communication) for fixed fees per contract period. Some offer an option to purchase set meals by mail; these programs are often advertised on popular television channels. Again, one should be reasonably sure they are sustainable for the long term, and best for you.

Vegetarian Considerations

Of interest is one other program that resembles the Pritikin Nutrition Regimen, but is vegetarian: that is the Dean Ornish vegetarian diet and wellness program. Like Pritikin's regimen (and my "Juan's Total Wellness for Over-75's" program), Dr. Ornish proposes an ultra-low-fat nutrition regimen *accompanied by at least half an hour of moderate exercise a day.* Dr. Ornish disallows all meats, fowl, and fish, as well as any oily foods such as nuts, olives, avocados; he also bans sugars (but not fruits). What he does allow are beans and other legumes, fruits, whole grains, and vegetables; and to a limited extent, some dairy products such as skim milk, egg whites, and nonfat yogurt. The hi-fiber caloric content of the Dean Ornish diet regimen is probably on the order of 10% to 15% fat, 15% to 20% protein, and the balance 65% to 75% carbs.

Like Pritikin's and "Juan's Total Wellness" programs, Dean Ornish advocates grazing, that is, snacking around mid-morning and mid-afternoon on low-calorie-density fillers: i.e. a bit of fruit, a cup of soup, a half slice of whole grain toast. The Ornish diet will also reduce weight IF, again, the individual exercises every day.

More importantly, Dr. Ornish's claim—based on medical

research (similar to Pritikin's UCLA-led research)—is that followers of his regimen significantly reduce the risk of heart disease and indeed, may reverse heart disease, cut the risk of cancer, and make diabetes and hypertension more manageable and even eliminate them.

There are two potential drawbacks to a completely vegetarian program in regard to nutrition for over-75's. Firstly, it is probably suitable only to a limited, smaller niche of those population groups simply because of lifetime choices and habit: most very elderly people will be unable to *totally* change their lifetime eating habits (becoming a vegetarian the Dr. Dean Ornish way requires *completely* changing, not just moderating, one's nutritional tastes and habits). Also, the vegetarian novice has to be careful to maintain the body's required nutrients so as not to become anemic or deficient in some essential body chemistry.

The other potential negative is that the Ornish program cuts out what are thought to be a few "good fats" from super-seniors' nutritional intake, which may be a disservice to some. Pritikin Logevity Center physicians, and other medical professionals (including physicians at the American Heart Association) have concluded that the omega-3 fatty acids in salmon and certain other oily fish, and the fat in nuts, are not only nutritious in themselves but help raise HDL healthy cholesterol levels that protect against coronary heart disease.

On balance, taking into account the lifetime habits of your super-senior parents and that population group as a whole (and considering you, too, now in your fifties and sixties), the moderated regimen that I have adopted and advocate is the optimum eating and nutrition program.

Example Eating Plans

So what might a typical two-week menu look like for, say, an over-75's super-senior couple electing to go for a supervised "total-immersion" program (say, either at home or on site at Juan's Wellness location) or at another off-site option such as a wellness spa? To break it down (three meals and two snacks a day) here is a sample—or typical—broad outline for illustration purposes (for actual recipes, see the last section of this book where some sixty examples are presented.)

Breakfasts are simple and mostly repetitive. Oatmeal in the morning is unsurpassed for daily health. I make my own oatmeal dry mix, enough for a couple of weeks, and keep it in a container (see the recipes' section following). I serve oatmeal four or five days of each week. Along with that, I suggest an assortment of berries, sliced apple, banana, and other fruit in three or four separate bowls for selection. Also, I offer whole grain toast (one half slice per person) along with a quarter-patty of butter and all-fruit jam, real coffee, real or herbal teas, and water. Plain, no-fat yogurt would be available, with a teaspoon of honey if desired. On days when no oatmeal is served, I prepare either two buckwheat pancakes (same amount of butter and honey) or scrambled egg or egg-beaters with stewed tomatoes and onion sauce, or Irish brown bread toasted and sugar-free marmalade, or (pre-rinsed) kippered herring with pan-seared half-tomato, roasted garlic, and capers.

A total immersion course involves two or three exercise sessions during the day, so appetites tend to be robust. After a healthy breakfast and forty-five minutes or an hour of exercise, a mid-morning snack is needed to get through to lunchtime without hunger pangs. Typical morning snacks that I would serve (selecting a different one every day) include: a large cup of vegetable and brown rice soup; a soft corn tortilla with guacamole; hummus and no-fat corn chips; small cup of turkey chili con carne; squash soup with salt-free whole-wheat crackers; an ounce of walnuts with a pear; crudités of celery, carrot, and zucchini with no-fat cheese dip; or black bean soup. Always, on the side, there would be a bowl of fresh fruit (oranges, apples, grapes, bananas) and a flask of hot water for herbal teas.

Lunch should be the main meal of the day; this works better for super-seniors and retirees. It's more difficult for working men and women to have their main meal in the middle of the day since the lunch break in the United States is often limited in time (unlike southern Europe and Latin America). The recipes' section lists over two-dozen main-course luncheon selections.

Every lunch should start with a large salad (dark leafy greens, tomato, carrot slivers, cucumber, diced apple, sweet onion, or other variations, with balsamic vinaigrette dressing), and a cup of soup. Entree proteins could consist of four to five-ounce flavor garnishes to accompany servings of vegetables and a complex carbohydrate. The garnish normally provides the name for the dish—such as "Madras Chicken Curry"—even though it should be the lesser part of the meal; that's due to tradition and the fact that in this country the protein is often the largest portion on the plate. Not so in the Orient.

I serve fish or seafood (four to five ounce portions) as the luncheon entre protein three times a week. Examples are "Roast Wild Skinless Salmon," "Pan Seared Skinless Bluefish Fillets," "Poached Halibut With Lemon Sauce," "Shrimp and Squid Okra Creole." I prepare fowl, such as chicken breast—skinless with all fat removed—sliced very thin with lemon, garlic, oregano, and fresh dill to form the basis for several variations. Lean white pork loin can be prepared as a base for dishes from the Far East, Near East, Latin America, and the Caribbean. Soy and seitan can be substituted for meat one or two days in a two-week period, as can other meatless dishes such as "Vegetable Ragout With Yams and Wild Rice," "Whole Wheat Penne with Tomatoes and Basil Sauce," and so on.

Lunches might be accompanied by a half slice of multi-grain bread, and concluded with a light dessert such as fruit salad, no-fat yogurt with berries, pear tart, Irish whiskey cake, or faux strawberry shortcake parfait.

Afternoon snacks would not resemble high tea at the Ritz (scones topped with strawberry jam and clotted cream, hot buttered crumpets dripping with syrup, little sandwiches loaded with egg salad and goose liver pate). Our afternoon snack is more like the morning snack: vegetable broth accompanied by corn chips, a cup of vegetable chili and cherry tomatoes, baked sweet potato half, small scoop of popcorn, crudité with a no-fat dip, and other options. Hot tea goes well in the afternoon. As always, a fruit bowl is available on the side.

Dinners should be lighter and, for super-seniors, eaten earlier. If the afternoon snack is taken at around 3 p.m., then older retirees or super-seniors should be ready for the evening meal from 5:30 p.m. to 6:30 p.m. As we get older we tend to eat earlier anyway; and in America our habits are inclined that way—that is, to eat a couple of hours earlier than families in Latin America and Southern Europe.

I'd encourage all to have another salad with or before their main supper course. Salads don't always have to be simply lettuce and tomato. A ring of peeled pear slices surrounding a bed of endives, radicchio, and arugula, with a few walnuts and slivers of figs on top (with a tablespoon of honeyed, balsamic vinegar) makes for a delicious alternative. There are scores of variations, all healthy.

The amount of food on one's supper plate should be two-thirds that of lunch, or less, because the meals would tend to be lighter dishes. Some of my supper recipe alternatives include scrambled egg-whites or egg-beaters heaped on a half-slice of whole grain toast or Irish brown bread, with a side of spinach or ratatouille. A light fish stew, in the center of a circle of brown rice, accompanied by pan-roasted zucchini and eggplant slices is another example. I might opt to serve Mexican Tamale Pie, infused with ground turkey breast, with black beans and thin-sliced French green beans. Or Asian dumplings, either vegetarian or with an ounce of diced chicken breast or minced shrimp, with brown rice noodles and Chinese cabbage. Once every two weeks, I make an exception and serve very-lean, dark meat such as roast venison accompanied by thick plum sauce and roast yams, peas, and pearl onions.

A glass of good red wine is allowed in the evening with dinner for those who enjoy wine. (The same health benefit can be gained from a glass of pure grape juice.)

These comprise a few examples of healthy meals and snacks that are nutritious, filling, and weight-reducing for those who need slimming. They are the sort of meals and the composition of food groups that—if prepared and partaken regularly—help to minimize the risk of incurring one of the mostly-avoidable maladies.

Other Considerations

The "Health Awareness" section in Chapter 6 consists of my notes from the series of occasional lectures by physicians and other professionals at my Wellness classes, plus a recap of findings from certain medical research studies summarizing benefits that seem to result from healthy and nutritious eating habits. For example, the onset of dementia may be slowed for those prone to early memory loss or mild cognitive impairment. Your healthy eating habits reduce the chances of incurring a serious fall. Anxiety symptoms may be moderated. Recovery from an illness or an operation, or a serious fall, is easier and faster.

Eating in not the most-healthy way may have been a lifelong habit for some. Super-seniors who are now in their mid 70's and early 80's may not be in the best shape to handle the physical problems that will eventually face them in their 90's, the ultra-senior years. Those habits CAN be modified (they do not have to be massively changed across the board) to redirect their future health to a more positive outlook, and at the same time revitalize their lives.

We can all grow older and live longer, and better. "Better" is the important word.

An important postscript for elders who are lactose intolerant and/or require gluten-free diets: all of Juan's recipes can be adapted to serve virtually identical-tasting meals and snacks to accommodate those restrictive dietary requirements. For lactose-free substitutions, replace skim milk with soy, rice or unsweetened almond milk (be careful about using too much soy). Instead of butter—the very limited amount we use anyway—substitute with an alternative such as Earth Balance. Instead of fat-free yogurt, use unsweetened soy yogurt.

Regarding gluten-free diets, instead of whole-wheat flours or pastas, use rice, cornmeal, or chestnut flours, and gluten-free brown rice and pastas. The packages are all marked clearly and most grocery stores now have a gluten-free section. You can even find a package of "gluten free baking mix" at Target, a great substitute for flours in any of these recipes. Since my wife and three daughters all have lactose-free and gluten free eating requirements, I have learned to make gluten-free, lactose-free griddlecakes that are better than pancakes one might get at the best of roadside diners.

Chapter 6.

Living Life Better

Pillar III: Health Awareness

Lecture Discussion Notes

Why add a "third pillar" of *Health Awareness* to a total wellness discipline? This chapter will motivate super-seniors—and you, their adult children (and/or caregivers)—to perform "doable exercises" and adopt an element of *extra* effort in following prudent and nutritious eating habits. The three pillars all tie together, and an awareness of, and interest in, health and disease-related issues is just as important an element as exercise and nutrition.

Many aging men die years before they should and earlier than their spouses (nursing homes and assisted living facilities usually have resident ratios of ten or more women to every three men). The reasons are in part because the men are either:

- Sedentary and have been lethargic since retirement
- Needlessly burdened with ominous bulk about the waist

- Unconcerned about geriatric health and wellness
- Inattentive to sensible nutrition and hydration

The average life expectancy in 2010 was 78, some 31 years longer than the average life expectancy at the beginning of the last century. These super-seniors are not necessarily living better. There are two million American ultra-seniors age 90 and above, whereas sixty years ago there were only twenty thousand. Yet these ultra-seniors often suffer from diseases such as hypertension, diabetes, arthritis, osteoporosis, or heart disease. Some are overweight, depressed, or take habit-forming drugs for anxiety. Many have artificial joints, and many require walkers or motorized wheelchairs.

Because a large number of post-75's seniors do not walk or exercise and have let their body-mass-index (BMI) numbers climb into the danger-zone, they become candidates for "the fall." After a serious fall, it can be a downhill slide, especially if—after a hospital stay—the subsequent nursing home or rehab center does not include a total wellness regimen encompassing physical therapy, plus sound nutrition, genuinely-compassionate care, and general health awareness education.

A surprisingly large segment of over-75's—whether in nursing homes or assisted-living facilities or even in their own homes—may be on as many as seven (or more) prescription drug medications. Apart from the potential for so many drugs having adverse interaction/s, it has been documented and published by medical research physicians that when an elderly person takes more than five or six prescription meds, the chances of incurring a serious fall increase dramatically, if not exponentially.

One way or another, post-75's men (those who make it into their 80's) die earlier than their brides; and surviving widows, in their 80's and 90's, may spend much of their time alone or experience feelings of isolation. The SSHG provides the basis for helping many of those seniors already over 75 or approaching that critical threshold—to live their extended lives longer and better.

My wellness and longevity regimen is obviously seeking to address the over-75's seniors themselves. However, my expectation is that those who work with the very elderly, the caregivers and geriatric specialists and professionals dedicated to looking after the old, and especially you—the adult children of super- and ultra-seniors—will welcome and benefit from the actionable disciplines herein, including the important "health awareness" discussion section introduced in the following pages.

The Issues

At "Juan's Total Wellness for Over-75's" classes, I encourage students and attending caregivers to subscribe to certain "health newsletters" disseminated by some of the larger medical schools, hospitals, and/or longevity clinics. Most major newspapers, such as the *Wall Street Journal* and the *New York Times*, have weekly subsections dealing with health and medical topics. There is also an array of reading materials and research summaries available on the Internet relating to almost every specific medical subject or disease.

In my Juan's Total Wellness classes, I sometimes bring in copies of health articles that I think will be of interest to the students. A discussion often ensues. The subject may be as varied as the attributes of Vitamin D to the possible causes of vertigo, or how to lower one's blood pressure through meditation and relaxation, or an author's story of how he or she coped with rehabilitation after a knee replacement.

Ideally once a quarter, I invite a guest lecturer—a medical specialist, family practice physician, emergency room doctor, a naturopathic doctor, chiropractic physician, or a nutritionist—to give a talk to the class on an issue or issues of particular interest to super-seniors. The lectures help to motivate super- and ultra-senior class attendees, give them encouragement to soldier on and, on occasion, to impart a bit of warning. A little fear is not necessarily a bad thing.

This chapter, the third pillar of "Juan's Total Wellness for Over-75's" is about becoming broadly familiar with the fundamentals of certain, mostly-avoidable maladies and their prevention and/or reversal.

The short subsections following comprise summaries of some of those talks. They may, additionally, contain extracted points and notes from a longevity clinic or a medical school's published newsletter/s, or from my own Juan's Wellness seasonal newsletters. These abbreviated subsections are intended to give a flavor of the health subjects and medical awareness issues that should be discussed with super- and ultra-seniors; and, perhaps even more importantly, that should be introduced to you who are in your fifties and sixties so that when you get to the same stage of elder life, you will be far more prepared than we ever were.

Notes From Talk 1: Anxiety and Depression in Aging

I invited a Family Practice Physician to share some of the latest research on depression and anxiety in order to help my class of super-seniors understand the subject better, since some of them did have relatives or friends with those symptoms.

The objectives of the presentation were to, firstly, impart a summary of treatment options for depression. The talk also touched on awareness of possible depression in oneself, family or friends, and knowing how best to prevent depression.

Everyone goes through satisfactory and even euphoric periods and then—at alternative times in life—through sad or traumatic periods. The good news is that the longer we live, the more content or happier we are likely to be. Mental health—in terms of mental satisfaction—generally improves with age. The not-so-good news is that some individuals, even at a relatively young age, can and do go through mild or severe depression.

Forms of depression include:

- Normal grief at the death of a friend or distant relative; short-lived depressive thoughts without disruption of one's life.

- Reactive depression precipitated by a severe event such as the death of a spouse or divorce; this may last longer than normal grief and may be disruptive to life and yet limited in duration to months rather than years.

- Dysthymia which is characterized by years of gloomy mood, causing behavioral sluggishness, guilt feelings, and self-criticism; Dysthymia can be so chronic, albeit relatively mild, that sufferers believe it is normal to feel that way—to outsiders it can seem to be part of their personality.

- Major depression: this involves feelings of anger, frustration, sadness, worthlessness, and hopelessness; the symptoms are not short lived. They interfere with normal living; they can degenerate into psychotic depression which has more severe symptoms associated with hallucinations and delusion.

- Vascular depression which involves depressive symptoms related to damage from vascular disease and is coupled to a slow but definite increase in cognitive impairment.

It's unlikely that anyone participating in wellness or exercise classes (such as in my "Juan's Total Wellness for Over-75's" program) would have forms of major depression, but all the definitions were reviewed for general interest in the subject, and—importantly—in order to lead to discussions of Vascular depression.

There are generally three theories revolving around the generic term depression—in regards to what is happening in the brain. First, stress seems to be a major player. If there is stress for a prolonged period, the brain shrinks resulting in a loss of nerve cells and their connections. Although unclear, this seems to affect certain glands and causes an imbalance of hormones. Exercise and intellectual stimulation contribute to an increase in "nourishment-chemicals" for the brain, which in turn counter the destructive effects of stress.

Secondly, genetics plays a role. People with a certain type of gene are more prone to depression than those with an alternate type of gene. However, as noted above, numerous studies have shown that exercise and diet as well as intellectual stimulation help to prevent depression regardless of the gene type.

Finally, blood vessels play a role; blood vessels of the brain can be affected by disease just as heart blood vessels are. Markers of inflammation have been found to be elevated in patients with depression. (It was also noted that severe depression appears to be an independent risk factor for heart disease, just as smoking and/or high LDL cholesterol are risk factors for heart disease.)

What causes depression?

- Major changes such as moving from one's longtime home of 50 years to a retirement community or assisted living facility
- Frustration over memory loss
- Chronic pain
- Certain prescription medications
- Isolation
- Poor diet
- Excessive alcohol intake
- Inactivity
- Insomnia

Depression and extreme stress can lead to loss of self-esteem or self-confidence and can induce fear or insecurity. However, I know many super-seniors—those in my Juan's Wellness classes and others at my elderly cousin's dementia unit—who have no symptoms of anxiety or depression. The counterpoint to anxiety or depression is happiness or contentment. Professional recommendations for maintaining contentment and a positive mental attitude—and warding off worry or mild depression—include:

- Developing new activities
- Making and maintaining new relationships/friends
- Being "social-minded"
- Adopting calming strategies such as joining a group

meditation, taking up yoga, tai chi, exercise class, cards or chorale

- Volunteering to help others
- Reducing fats and sugars (minimizing fats and sugars in one's diet can improve mental disposition and help ward off worry)

The results of countless studies and surveys dealing with this subject can be found on the Internet. One European study on the impact of exercise vis-à-vis depression found that a group of women who attended yoga class three times a week, over a period of several months, improved their depression-test-scores by 50%. As a bonus, regular exercise also reduced their complaints regarding chronic pain.

Multiple studies have found that tai chi has been instrumental in reducing anxiety, stress, and depression. A 2008 study concluded that mindfulness-based cognitive therapy, MBCT, was just as effective as anti-depressant drugs in the treatment and prevention of depression and in warding off potential relapse into depression; in this case a Buddhist form of meditation was utilized to focus patients on the present rather than let them dwell on past or possible future worries.

A Scandinavian study found that people with positive and/or strong social connections and relationships were much less likely to suffer cognitive impairment than those who were reclusive or lacked social skills. A separate similar study in the Far East arrived at the same conclusion. All of these studies related to depression and anxiety yielded results and conclusions that seem to suggest that the highest levels of happiness or contentment are brought about by attributes of compassion, empathy and in helping others.

Returning to nutrition and diet, several independent studies have shown the so-called Mediterranean diet reduces inflammation, which has a role in vascular diseases of the heart and of the brain. This diet has many similarities to the healthy nutrition guidelines espoused in my "Juan's Total Wellness for Over-75's" program; namely, it is a diet rich in fruit, vegetables, legumes, fish, and whole grains—with moderate use of virgin olive oil and white meats—and minimal intake of processed sugars, fatty foods, white flours and rice, and red meat.

Highlighting the positive and concluding on a high note, the optimum levels of contentment and happiness in super- and ultra-seniors are brought about by the attributes of compassion, empathy, and in service to others. Those attributes may be enhanced by the camaraderie of participation—participation in mild exercise programs such as described in this SSHG and involvement in learning more about the issues of health, diseases, and nutrition.

Notes From Talk 2: Before And After The Serious Fall

We all fall, some more than others. A toddler discovering his newfound mobility falls frequently, yet rarely gets injured. When an older person falls, injury is more common. Sometimes a fall can alter your lifestyle.

As one ages, normal changes occur in the body. Several organ systems conspire to make super- and ultra-seniors more vulnerable. The neurologic system, i.e. the brain, nerves, and sensory organs, suffers from slowed reflexes and reaction time, decreased sense of joint position (critical to balance), and erosion of vision (particularly in poor light environments). In the muscular skeletal system, bone density and muscle strength decline. These two system changes result in less agile coordination and reduced ability to compensate for sudden stress placed on the body. For example, missing a curb edge results in a fall and weakened bone structure results in a fracture.

When illness impacts older people's organ systems, they become even more impaired (resulting in an increased propensity to fall). Emergency department doctors often find that urinary tract infection, pneumonia, congestive heart failure, or poorly controlled diabetes comprise the inciting cause behind a fall. Medications used to treat disease can have unfortunate side affects, resulting in a serious fall. Multiple drugs can impair cognition, balance, or the cardiovascular system's ability to maintain proper blood pressure control. The rate of hospitalization for hip fractures after a fall (based on 1996 centers for disease control, CDC, data) was far greater for women than for men.

Where are people likely to fall? For super-seniors, 60% of falls occur where they live; of the balance, 30% of falls occur in public places (shops, malls, theatres, churches, etc.) and 10% occur in nursing homes or hospitals.

How frequently do super- and ultra-seniors fall? In any given year, an average of 30%-plus will have a mild or serious fall. Most of the falls are not serious, but medical attention is required 20% of the time. Of those seeking medical attention, just 10% will have had a fall serious enough to result in a fracture.

"De-conditioning" of one's body is the lingering effect of illness on the body which results in loss of muscle mass and reduced mobility of joints. A flu-like illness, for instance, that keeps an ultra-senior in bed for a couple of days may cause lingering changes to the muscular skeletal system that can take weeks to regain. Though the cough may have resolved, muscle strength and coordination are still recovering.

Alcohol—alone or in combination with prescription drugs—is a significant factor in the cause of falls. The blunting of the neurologic system by alcohol consumption need not be at intoxication levels to cause falls. One or two drinks on a good day may not cause a problem vis-à-vis balance or coordination; but when combined with recent illness, adverse environmental conditions, or prescription medication, the total affect could be dramatic.

Not all falls in older people result in serious injury, but five to 15% is significant enough. The most common major injuries, by far, comprise fractures (hip, shoulder, arm and so on), followed by head trauma. Hip fractures occur in one to two percent of all falls. The consequences of hip fractures are significant: hospitalization stays are, on average, one week and 25% will require nursing/rehab-home placement for an extended period of time. More than half will experience restricted mobility. Most importantly, the psychological impact of a fall should not be underestimated; the fear of falling again and a lack of self-confidence can lead to unnecessary restriction of activities followed by further decline. This is where "the awareness" of such potential consequences or after-effects (of a fall, for example) can help super- and ultra-seniors to get over a shattered confidence level much faster than otherwise. A Total Wellness program rebuilds and helps to maintain self-confidence, in addition to the strengthening and balance/posture emphasis.

Super-seniors can do a lot to prevent falls and/or minimize potential injury. Physical activity is important. Failure to exercise regularly results in poor muscle tone, decreased strength and loss of bone mass and flexibility. Any exercise program that is regularly followed and challenges endurance, strength, and flexibility will reduce the risk of a serious fall and improve the chances of avoiding serious injury.

Diet, of course, is also important. The vitality of muscles and bones depends on a well balanced diet. The progression of chronic illness is impacted by what one eats.

Polypharmacy, the use of multiple medications, is increasingly common as people age and accumulate medical conditions. The more drugs taken, the greater the chance for side effects and interactions.

Falls will happen, but we can minimize the risk. The best advice is: exercise, eat well, and we will all be stronger and safer.

A Talk About The Relationship Of Foods We Eat and Functioning Of The Brain

Growing up, my mother told me, "Eat your broccoli; it's food for the brain." Now science and the medical profession endorse this intuitive knowledge long held by our grandparents and parents.

Research studies over the past decade in the US and in Europe indicate that diet has significant impact on cognitive function. Changes in dietary habits have long been known to improve cardiovascular disease through their impact on elevated cholesterol, high blood pressure, and/or diabetes. A healthy, balanced diet works on brain vessels to prevent stroke; and—importantly—sound nutrition can improve your brain's ability to function normally.

Doctors now know that older people with a particular dietary history have been found to show lower rates or levels of decline in cognitive functions, such as memory retention, daily living activities, and problem solving. They have also experienced reduced occurrence of brain lesions.

What is considered normal aging of the brain depends on several factors:

- Healthy older people can have mild declines in visual or verbal memory, and in their ability to recall names of people and find objects or words.
- Verbal reasoning and vocabulary can remain unchanged or even improve with age.

However, when cognitive changes are abrupt and/or result in social problems, we begin to approach a loosely defined condition termed Minimal Cognitive Impairment (MCI). An example of this could include a pattern of forgetting near-term things that one would typically remember (but activities of daily living, judgment, and reasoning skills are not necessarily affected). Once independent living, or complex thinking is affected, the diagnosis of dementia (AD) or vascular dementia (VaD) is entertained.

The cause of AD or VaD remains unclear. Multiple factors may be involved. Patients with AD have brain lesions called amyloid plaques and tangle. Reduced blood flow to parts of the brain is believed to cause VaD. A significant number of recent international and US studies have focused on food association with brain function, with sometimes surprising results.

A Chicago study of over-65 year olds conducted from the late 1990's to 2005 associated fish consumption at least once a week with a 10% per year reduced decline of cognitive function. The overall impact was equivalent to being three to four years younger in cognitive age compared to those who did not consume fish once a week.

(The impact is due to the beneficial aspects of Omega-3 oil found in fatty fish such as salmon.)

A 2007 study published in the US regarding the effects of diet on genetically modified mice that developed brain lesions (similar to the plaques and tangles seen in human AD patients) found that when the mice were fed food similar in composition to the typical American diet—i.e. high in omega-6 fatty acids—they had greater evidence of brain lesions than when fed a favorable diet—i.e. low omega-6 and high in omega-3 fatty acids.

A 2007 study in France of 8,000 over-65's concluded that diets that included fish once a week, plus fruits and vegetables on a daily basis, and used oils high in omega-3 and low in omega-6 reduced their association with dementia by 28-40% over a four-year period.

A US study (completed in 2006) followed 2,200 people with an average age of 70 and concluded that those who ate a "Mediterranean diet" were less likely to develop AD. The greater the adherence to the so-called Mediterranean diet, the greater the cognitive benefit. The improvement ranged from 10% to 40%. (The Mediterranean diet comprised high intake of certain foods: i.e. fruits including apples, oranges, grapefruit, peaches, apricots, plums, bananas; salads and vegetables including tomatoes, broccoli, cabbage, chard, cauliflower, brussel-sprouts, raw or cooked carrots, corn, yams, spinach, collard greens, yellow squash; legumes including peas, lima beans, lentils, beans; carbs including oatmeal, dark bread, brown rice/ pasta, potatoes; and mono-unsaturated fatty acids, such as found in olive oil. The Mediterranean diet also included moderate amounts of fish, low intake of meat, low to moderate amounts of dairy and a limited amount of red wine.)

An Italian study, published in 2007, followed 1,445 over-65-year-olds for almost four years and found that consumption of one alcoholic drink a day (mostly red wine) slowed the progression of MCI (mild cognitive impairment) by 85%. Higher amounts of alcohol showed little additional advantage.

Another study conducted in France (from 2003 to 2007) of 7,000 over-65's women who drank three or more cups of coffee or tea per day had slower rate of decline in cognitive function. The measurable improvement factors ranged from 30 to 70%.

A six-year study completed in the US in 2006 of 3,718 over-65's found that those who ate three servings of vegetables a day enjoyed a 40% slower rate of cognitive decline. This was equated as being about five cognitive-years younger than the "low-vegetable-consuming" group.Dark, green leafy vegetables had the greatest beneficial association.

In 2001, a Swedish group reported on 400 over-75's who had been closely observed for three years. Those people with low blood levels of B12 or folate were twice as likely of being diagnosed with AD three years later. The risk was greatest for people deficient in both B12 and folate. B12 is found in foods such as fish, meat, and dairy products; while rich sources of folate are found in spinach, peas, and grains.

The general conclusion from these and other international and US studies indicates that prudent nutrition (as advocated in "Juan's Total Wellness for Over-75's" nutrition section earlier) may indeed help slow the onset of gradual decline in cognitive functions as we get older.

So, eat smart:

- Consume wild-caught fish (especially salmon) and lots of fruits, salads, vegetables, and legumes.
- Lower intake of Omega-6 fatty foods and oils.
- Avoid all junk and processed foods.
- Minimize salt, sugars, and red meats.
- Eat whole grain breads, oatmeal, bran, and brown rice.

Notes From an Article I Wrote For a Quarterly, "Juan's Wellness" Newsletter

Essential fatty acids (certain oils and fats in food) may be sub-categorized as "most-essential" fatty acids, "essential" fatty acids, and "partially-essential" fatty acids. The most-essential fatty acids are Omega 3 (known as LNA); essential fatty acids are Omega 6 (known as LA); and partially-essential fatty acids are Omega 9 (which become essential only if not enough Omega 3 and Omega 6 are obtained through one's diet).

Earlier studies have indicated that most Americans consume over twelve times as much Omega 6 as Omega 3 fatty acids in their diets. Some nutritionists advocate a more acceptable ratio as being on the order of four times as much Omega 6 as Omega 3 in the average daily diet. For a healthy and nutritious diet—such as we advocate in many of our week-long "Juan's Total Wellness" recipe plans—one needs to get about 1.5 to 2.0 ounces (40 to 55 grams) of Omega 3 and 6 essential fatty acids in the average daily diet.

Some examples of healthy source foods for most-essential and essential fatty acids are as follows:

Omega 3's (most-essential)—wild salmon, albacore tuna, skinless bluefish, and cleaned mackerel fillets; walnuts and Brazil nuts (1 ounce servings a day); avocado and broccoli; dark leafy vegetables such as chard, spinach, kale, and collards; and cold-pressed flaxseed oil and canola oil.

Omega 6's (essential)—skinless chicken breast, white meat pork (4 ounce portions only), olives, pine nuts, and extra virgin olive oil (first pressed).

I always propose to class attendees that they should try to have "good" fish three times a week, copious servings of dark leafy vegetables, and limit the use of cooking oil—as in sautéing or searing—to extra virgin olive oil in very moderate amount/s.

That brings us to fats. The percentage of fat in our average daily diet should be no more than 20% of caloric intake. Fat content in the average American's typical daily diet is, or was, above 35% according to a 1994 study—it may be higher now. The typical U.S. daily diet comprises 35% fat, 15% protein, 50% carbohydrate. What the numbers *should* be for a healthier nation (re a "typical" daily diet) would be more like 20% fat (mostly "good" fats), 20% proteins (of the type/s advocated by "Juan's Wellness"), 60% carbohydrates (rich in fiber and unrefined grains).

Breaking down the average daily caloric content in an eating plan for a small/medium-build man weighing, say, 155 pounds who is 5 foot 10 inches tall, with a BMI of 23, could be roughly as follows: fat 425 calories; protein 425 calories; carbohydrate 1,250 calories . . . plus 100 calories for a four ounce glass of red wine . . . for a total of 2,200 calories per day. An active woman weighing 130 pounds could consume about 10% to 12% less across the board, for an average daily caloric content of circa 2,000 calories. Larger body frame men and women could require more calories.

The average caloric intake examples may seem low to the typical American consumer. It might suggest that the person/s involved must be constantly hungry. Not necessarily so. With the right foods at meal times—including mid-morning and mid-afternoon snacks— based on smaller protein portions, limited whole grains and nutritious carbohydrates, and large amounts of vegetables, salads and fruits which are all very low in caloric-density, the healthy consumers are never "hungry"; they are continuously and comfortably sated.

An example of an evening meal providing essential fatty acids together with abundant volume, thus providing appetite-satisfaction and moderate calorie-density, is this "Juan's Total Wellness" menu favorite, Seared Wild Salmon: pan-seared, skinless, wild-caught salmon with lemon, garlic, dill, and tarragon and a thin sugar-free marmalade or chutney glazing; steamed, chopped chard with pine nuts; yams, carrots, and parsnips mashed together; a "tricolor" salad of radicchio, endive, and Boston bib lettuce with sliced pears, tomato, and red pepper, sprinkled with non-dairy, no-fat "mozzarella" and walnuts, and a simple dressing of the very best balsamic vinegar.

To prepare the above, have a large, cast iron pan very hot with one teaspoon of EVOO before setting in the salmon (cut into 5-ounce pieces, top side down), marinated with marmalade glaze and lined with ultra thin lemon slices. When you turn the salmon, after about four minutes, the top surfaces will be partially blackened. Cook the other sides for about two to three minutes; sprinkle herbs and minced garlic about the sides of the fish on to the hot pan. Serve all very hot with the green vegetables and pureed yams/carrot mash and a wedge of lemon on each plate. Have the individual large salad bowls to the side. A glass of California pinot noir or a good, French burgundy is a nice accompaniment, and ice water.

Notes From My Research Into MCI: Mild (or Minimal) Cognitive Impairment

I began a study of MCI and one of the drugs often prescribed to alleviate MCI and Alzheimer's disease because my elderly cousin, Geraldine, was diagnosed with MCI six years ago. She was put on the maximum dosage of a drug, Aricept, and the side effects were intolerable. I took her off the drug. However, I had a continuing disagreement with the neurologist and neuro-psychologist who had diagnosed Geraldine, as I did not feel she was demented or sufficiently forgetful to warrant such a powerful medication. As it turns out, the drug in question is only useful for eighteen months to two years. If it was ever to be needed by Geraldine, it was started at least six years prematurely.

This article, therefore, is a cautionary tale. You should look carefully into the prescription drugs your parents are taking, and get further (second) opinions from your family practice doctor/s regarding the potential interactions between medications, and/or the real need for some of them.

Aricept (Donepezil) is a drug manufactured by the Eisai Pharmaceutical Company of Japan, marketed in the USA by Pfizer. It was being promoted in television ads as suitable for all phases of Alzheimer's disease (the manufacturer's brochure indicates it is *"for the treatment of mild to moderate Alzheimer's"*).

Medicare includes Aricept in its coverage for the Part D Drug

Prescription Program as a "non-preferred brand" (i.e. with no lower cost or generic status). In England, however, the UK National Health Service (NICE) does not cover Aricept's cost.

Aricept has been found by the University of Oxford, in a 2006 study, as having "results that show some improvement in global clinical state," regarding to Alzheimer's. However, it also concluded that "a variety of adverse effects were recorded . . . the debate on whether Donepezil is effective continues . . . there is no evidence that Donepezil delays the onset of Alzheimer's."

A second major study by the University of Oxford (2006), in regard to Aricept vis-à-vis Mild (or Minimal) Cognitive Impairment (MCI), concluded that "there is no consensus on diagnostic criteria for MCI—[which] remains a vague term . . . there is no evidence to support the use of Donepezil for patients with MCI . . . there are significant adverse side effects."

Other studies have concluded that Aricept may be effective for eighteen months to two years only, a conclusion supported by Pfizer's own research.

The pertinent question for seniors, and their relatives or mentors, is: when is the right time to take Aricept? The elderly person's primary care physician might make an analysis as to interaction between Aricept and other prescription drugs. For example, interaction between Aricept and Toprol may slow heart rate; between Aricept and Zoloft may affect liver function, and so forth.

With today's heavy advertising of blockbuster prescription drugs on television and elsewhere, with the often repeated phrase, "*ask your doctor if this drug is right for you*," both the elderly and their doctors may be unknowingly bending to sales' pressure/s, thus lowering the bar on accepting an attitude of a "more-than-necessary" intake of prescriptions drugs.

In a *New Yorker* article, "The Way We Age Now," April 30, 2007, Dr. Atul Gawande points out, "The three primary risk factors for falling are poor balance, taking more than four prescription medications, and muscle weakness." Recent studies show that 350,000 Americans fall and break a hip each year. Before accepting a new prescription drug such as Aricept (especially high initial dosage) from a neurologist (on the basis of a neuropsychologist's recommendation), a careful analysis and discussion between the patient (including his or her responsible individual, relative, or spouse) and the patient's primary care physician, regarding all medications as well as the timetable-related necessity of taking the new drug, may be the most prudent procedure.

Be careful, do research, talk it over—and be sure.

Chapter 7.

Where to go from here? Next Steps

The Hardest Part Is Getting Someone You Love Started

I have talked to many good friends, and even more of my local acquaintances, about starting an exercise routine with me—without ever seeing them in one of my classes. Some folk brush off the suggestion with repartee and a laugh; others say, "I'll be there, one of these days."

Of the men and women who do join my classes, most have been encouraged to do so by their adult children. Once begun, the class routine and camaraderie prove to be infectious, and those new super-senior attendees stay the course for a year or more. The question you are undoubtedly asking is: "How do *I* get my super-senior parent/s to begin this regimen—or at least some of it—at home?" First, discuss the general tone and outline of this book, *Wellness For Super-Seniors* with them. Talk about the Three Pillars of a total wellness program and stress that—in regard to the exercises sector—nothing is difficult or painful. Point out the exercises can be done sitting if necessary, or standing using the back of a chair for support and balance, or a blend of both. Explain isometrics, and tell them there are no machines or bands or equipment needed for these exercises— and no lying prone or sitting on a mat on the floor.

Pick out three or four exercises from the list of "A Typical 50-Minute Class Routine" as presented in chart form on the following pages, and do them with your parents. You will be able to gradually add more exercises, and eventually they will do the whole routine on their own a few times a week. By that time you will have been able to talk nutrition, suggest what to avoid and what to eat, and they will have read this book themselves.

Here are the exercises I would suggest starting off with. Always begin with easy deep breathing, lifting the elbows or arms on an inhale, and lowering them on an exhale—repeat that five times. Then it's important to stretch the lower legs (calves and tendons); if your parents are able to stand, have them raise up on their toes and hold for a few seconds, then lower and repeat. If sitting, raise the heels up, hold them there, and lower them again. Next I would have them do easy squats, not going down too far, holding the position for a count of five, and returning to the standing position. If your parents are not able to stand but are sitting, have them raise their legs to the horizontal, hold them there, then lower them—this strengthens the big quadriceps muscles in a similar manner to squats. Strengthening the legs is extremely important for super-seniors in order to improve balance and minimize the chances of incurring a fall.

Next, I would have your parents do a couple of the arm and shoulder isometrics, clearly shown on the diagrams in Chapter 8. And finally, two exercises for the lower back and core (waist, pelvis, abdomen)— these are vital for super-seniors who are experiencing lower back pain and who are continually bent over in an uncomfortable walking position. My two exercises for the lower back, done in a standing position, are the equivalent of two exercises—"Pelvic Tilt" and "Traction"—that are normally done prone in gyms and physical therapy clinics.

Those few starting exercises should take no more than ten minutes. Within two weeks you will be up to twenty minutes, then half an hour—and then, your parents may be willing to continue on their own.

As you gradually expand your discussions about exercise and its benefits, you will naturally begin to talk about nutrition and health issues, particularly if you have left a copy of *Wellness For Super-Seniors* with your parents and they have glanced through it from time to time. The book should be used as a reference manual. Adjustments to eating habits only need to be encouraged early on if your parent (one or both) have obvious problems relating to certain health issues, such as diabetes type 2, high blood pressure, prior heart disease, high cholesterol, or excess weight. There is a one-page tear-out sheet a little further on that lists, in summary form, the foods to concentrate on, and the fats and sugars and salts that super-seniors should try to minimize, or at least reduce.

To a normal-weight person—one who exercises moderately and whose body-mass-index is below 25—the business of eating sensibly and keeping trim seems simple. And the payoff for that build of person is that it is much easier to move around, to accomplish tasks, and to not find oneself quickly fatigued or exhausted. But for the considerably overweight people—even though they know all of the above and realize that they would feel so much better and more energized if they weighed less—it is still extraordinarily difficult to begin a new eating regimen.

Nevertheless, you have to keep trying. And so do your parents. It's worth it. On the next two pages you'll find "Home Reminder Sheets" that will help you as you work up to a twenty minute routine and begin discussing nutrition with your parents. Cut them out or copy them and attach them to the kitchen message board or refrigerator door; that's what my class students are asked to do, and it serves as a constant reminder to eat right and not forget about regular exercise.

A HOME REMINDER EXERCISE PROGRAM
EASY WORKOUT FOR 20 MINUTES

- **Breathing.** Start with two sets (five each) of <u>deep</u> breathing to freshen and loosen up. Thumbs under chin, elbows up, in through nose and out through mouth.

- **Leg Muscle Stretches.** Fingers lightly on a counter or back of chair for balance. Think POSTURE. First do two sets (five each) of up-on-toes; hold it for count of five, to stretch lower calf. Then do one set (five times) of mid calf stretch, left foot forward first and right back, go down a third of the way keeping back leg straight and heel on the floor: Hold for count of five. Switch legs.

- **Squat.** Feet shoulder width apart. Stand TALL. Go down one third of the way (or whatever comfortable) with fingers on chair or on thighs/quads. Hold for five seconds. Repeat five times.

- **Lower Back Pelvic Tilt.** Stand TALL, hands on upmost part of glutes, press in hard while tightening tummy/abs muscles, tightening buttocks/glutes and picture "tilting" the pelvis to more correct position: Then rotate five time left, five times right, while maintaining pressure on lower back.

- **Lower Back & Spine Traction.** Stand TALL. Hands on upper thighs. Press in to one self while tightening tummy/abs muscles. Do the same rotations, while maintaining the pressure.

This will stretch your spine up and help straighten your posture.

• **Arms, Shoulders, Back & Upper Chest.** Do both Tension and Pressure exercises by firstly clenching fingers together and pulling apart; then by placing fist in the palm and pushing together. Alternate with five sets of each, and rotate five times each side while holding the strain. Stand TALL throughout the isometric exercises.

• If time still permits, do Biceps and Triceps exercises, boxing position, with Tension and Pressure against your own self.

• Constantly think about POSTURE. Try to straighten up, walk tall.

DAILY NUTRITION TIPS

- A breakfast of good cereal (oatmeal or a rough low-sugar dry cereal), fruit/berries, whole wheat or multigrain toast, coffee ok.

- A mid-a.m. snack, if time permits, e.g. a cup of broth, fruit like pear or orange or banana, some corn chips and hummus, other soup, etc.

- For main meals (noon and/or evening) try to have copious salad, vegetables, legumes; and for starches preferably browns or reds (brown rice, pasta, yams, etc); with smaller portions proteins like fish (wild salmon, other wild caught fish or shellfish—not farmed), skinless chicken breast, white meat pork. Minimize red meat (ok on occasion). Soups to start are good. A glass of wine or two is ok, as is a cocktail if you are used to that. Fruits are great. Minimize rich cream desserts, chocolate black forest cake and the like (sometimes ok, of course).

- Try for a mid afternoon snack as well: Cup of tea, crackers, a healthy cookie.

- Late night snack, if watching movie: popcorn without oleo or butter or salt.

- Think about **BALANCE**, daily. Walking better and taller, exercising frequently, and eliminating floor-clutter will lessen the chance of a fall.

A TYPICAL 50-MINUTE SEQUENCE

Class Handout (*Refer to the exercises in Chapter 8 to follow along*)

1. BREATHING (deep)

In through nose, full exhalation (pursed lips), elbows up/down,

5 times

Repeat 3 sets; on 3rd set, raise arms overhead and stretch on inhale

2. LOWER BODY (for legs/ankles/feet)

a) Toes (stretch lower calf) 5 times: 2 sets

b) Dips: right leg foreword, left leg back (stretch mid calf), 5 times

Switch feet, repeat

c) Squats (strengthen quads), 5 times: 3 sets

On 3rd set, rotate side to side

3. CORE (for lower back/stomach)

a) Fore/aft bends (warm up lower spine)

5 times

b) Pelvic tilt with side to side rotation (firm abs and glutes)

5 times

c) Traction (hands on upper thighs) with rotation side to side

5 times

d) Abs strengthen (thumbs on belly button w/ rotation, firm abs)

5 times

4. UPPER BODY (for arms/chest/shoulders)

a) Biceps (right arm then left arm)

Fist up, pulling in; with other hand inside wrist, resisting

Rotate 5 times side to side

b) Triceps (right arm then left arm)

Fist up, pushing out; with other hand outside wrist, resisting

Rotate 5 times side to side

c) Upper Chest Pressure

Fist in palm, position hands by belly button, press and rotate

5 times side to side

d) Upper Chest Tension

Hook fingers, position hands by belly button, pull apart and rotate 5

times side to side

e + f) Same as c & d BUT with arms overhead for rotations (difficult,

see images)

5. HEAD/NECK

a) Interlace fingers behind head, press gently

Rotate 5 times side to side

b) Right heel of hand on right temple

Press gently for count of 5, for 5 times

c) Left heel of hand on left temple

Press gently for count of 5, for 5 times

Note: grimace face/mouth during above exercises (see image)

6. WARM UP FOR AEROBICS

Warm up legs again with

a) 'Up-On-Toes' 5 times: 1 set and

b) 'Squats' 5 times: 1 set

7. AEROBICS

a) Legs out to side (inner thigh strength/aerobic warm up)

Right leg out 5 times, then

Left leg out 5 times

b) Legs out to rear (hamstring strength, lower back stretch & aerobic)

Right leg back 5 times, then

Left leg back 5 times

c) Aerobic Slow March: 50 left-right steps; raise legs high, slow cadence

d) Aerobic Fast March: 50 left-right steps; smaller leg raises, fast cadence

8. COOL DOWN

Slowly shake limbs and loosen any remaining tight spots

Sit on a chair and breathe deeply and slowly for 5 times, with eyes closed

Note: Refer to the images in the exercise section to help learn sequence

Finally, LET ME REPEAT: Yes, You Can

Adopting a new wellness program that involves regular, structured exercise and a modified diet regimen *on your own* is, of course, more challenging than being a member of a group class—both as to starting and in keeping it up. The advantages of joining a scheduled class are obvious:

- Set days and times of the week
- Same classmates and repartee and accompanying camaraderie
- Personal encouragement from instructor
- Reminder handouts and "homework"
- On-site lectures to reinforce goals

We *can* duplicate those advantages with this book as an aid. Remember, no super-senior who is at home alone should be exercising alone, unless he is in his seventies, or early-eighties, *and* is active and fairly strong and has good balance. For beginners to this Juan's Wellness regimen who are home alone, however, and who are not quite so sure of their balance and/or state of fitness (or who may be on multiple medications), they *should* be joined in their initial months' exercise routines by you, the adult son or a daughter, or under the supervision of a caregiver, a personal fitness coach or a fitness-qualified friend.

In order to further facilitate "at-home" individuals keeping up with Juan's Total Wellness regimen (exercises *and* nutrition, as well as with general health tips)—I do provide constant encouragement and advice, with a number of *at-home* digital aids that I have developed over the past several year. Use them, and you and your parents will succeed. They will be revitalized. *Be convinced; you can do this!*

Super-Seniors (clockwise): Frank, 95; Betty-Ann, 95; Jack, 97; Connie, 90.

Chapter 8.

Juan's Total Wellness 50 Exercises

Section Contents and Introduction

An important point to remember is to set a fixed time each day (for four or five days of the week) to conduct your exercise routine. Whether it's seven a.m. before breakfast, or mid-morning, or late afternoon, block it out and dedicate the precious minutes to your physical wellbeing. You need just ten minutes at first; then slowly build up to 40 minutes per day over a period of four months. Do the same with the level of effort you exert—begin easy without using a lot of strength on the isometric exercises, or bending or dipping too deep on the stretch exercises. In due course, sooner than you would expect, you will find yourself exerting more and more tension and pressure without resorting to stress or pain, and you will notice new strength and improved balance within two to three months.

You need no props, and you can be anywhere to perform these routines. Make sure you have two chairs handy, one for balance (holding the chair-back) and one for resting. Or, you can use a counter top for balance if you are in the kitchen area.

Do only those exercises that are depicted with an asterisk if you are a super-senior or ultra-senior. The exercises marked "Advanced" are considerably more difficult, and are meant for 'junior-seniors' in the 55 to 75 age brackets. The list of Juan's Fifty Exercises is presented in the following pages.

JUAN'S 50 EXERCISES

Exercise Descriptions, Anatomical Sectors and Illustrative Photos:

i) **WARM UPS** 79

deep-breathing, limbs' loosening

ii) **LOWER BODY STRENGTHENING** 81

ankles, tendons, calves, quads and hamstrings

iii) **UPPER BODY STRENGTHENING** 86

biceps, triceps, shoulders and chest

iv) **HEAD & NECK STRENGTHENING** 91

facial muscles, tendons, upper neck vertebrae

v) **CORE BODY STRENGTHENING** 94

lower back muscles and lower vertebrae, abdominals, waist

vi) **AEROBIC BODY STRENGTHENING** 100

to raise heart rate, work legs and arms

vii) **COOL DOWN** 103

slow heart rate to normal, relax and meditate

The exercises with an asterisk are part of a typical 50 minute Juan's Wellness class.

WARM UPS

1. Deep Inhale/Exhale Bellows *

Interlace fingers and place thumbs under your chin, with elbows together in front of your chest.
Raise elbows to the side on a deep inhale through your nose.
Fully exhale through pursed lips while lowering elbows.

Repeat 5 times: Do 2 sets.

Warms up body, loosens shoulders.

WARM UPS

2. Deep Inhale/Exhale *
with arms stretch

Raise arms overhead on an inhale,
Stretch to the sky.
Slowly lower arms while exhaling
through pursed lips.

Repeat 5 times: Do 1 set.

Warms up body, stretches core, improves posture.

3. Shoulder Rolls *
with wrists shake-out

Roll your shoulders forward and back.
Shrug, loosen joints, and wiggle wrists.

Continue for 10 seconds:
Repeat 2 times.

Loosens shoulders and wrists.

LOWER BODY STRENGTHENING

4. Tiptoe Stretch & Balance *

Hold counter top or chair back lightly
for balance.
Rise up on tiptoes, and hold for 5
seconds:
Then resume standing position.

Repeat 5 times: Do 2 sets.

*Stretches lower calf muscles, helps posture
and balance.*

5 & 6. Mid Calf Stretch *
left & right

Hold counter top or chair back for
balance.
Place left leg back, straight,
bending right knee.
Keep left heel on floor—
(feel stretch in left calf).
Hold the stretch for 5 seconds.
Rise up.
Repeat 5 times.
Switch legs; repeat 5 times on the
other side.

Do 1 set for each side.

Stretches mid-calf and lower back

LOWER BODY STRENGTHENING

7. Quads Squat *

Place hands on top of quads during squat, or on chair back for balance.
Place feet shoulder-width apart, and sink down one-third of the way.
Hold position for 5 seconds.
Rise up to standing position.

Repeat 5 times: Do 2 sets.

Strengthens quads, hamstrings, and calf muscles.

8. Quads Squat *
with rotations

Place hands on top of quads, and slowly lower into a squat position (1/3 to half squat, or less, according to comfort). Slowly rotate 15 degrees to the right, then 15 degrees to the left, for 5 full rotations.

Do 1 set.

Strengthens quads, hamstrings, and abdominal muscles.

LOWER BODY STRENGTHENING
Note: The next five 'lower' exercises are much more difficult and are meant for advanced students.

9. Quad Squat March
and march slow in place
(aerobic/advanced)

Place one or both hands on a chair back or counter top.
Squat down to one-third (or less) dip.
Begin slow cadence march, 2 paces per second.
Continue for up to 20 full double-paces.

Do 1 set.

Strengthens quads, improves balance.

10. Quad Squat March
and march fast in place
(aerobic/advanced)

Place one or both hands on chair back or counter top.
Squat down to one-third (or less) dip.
Begin double-time cadence march, 4 paces per second.
Continue for up to 50 full double-paces.

Do 1 set.

Strengthens quads, hamstrings, and calf muscles.

LOWER BODY STRENGTHENING

11. Quad Squat Thigh Press *with rotations* (advanced)

Place feet shoulder-width apart; sink into squat position.
Place hands on mid-thighs.
Press hands hard down on thighs, maintain pressure.
Rotate 20 degrees to each side, slowly.

Make 5 full rotations: Do 1 set.

Strengthens all lower leg muscles and abdomen.

12. Quad Squat Hamstring Pull *with rotations* (advanced)

Place feet shoulder-width apart; sink into squat position.
Place hands under mid-thighs, and pull up hard.
Maintain tension against hamstrings.
Rotate 20 degrees to each side, slowly.

Make 5 full rotations: Do 1 set.

Strengthens quads, hamstrings, lower leg and foot muscles.

LOWER BODY STRENGTHENING

13. Deep Squat Tension *with rotations* (advanced)

Place feet shoulder-width apart.
Sink into very deep squat (most difficult position).
Press down on mid-quads and Rotate 20 degrees to each side, slowly.

Make 5 full rotations: Do 1 set.

Strengthens quads, hamstrings, ankles and calf muscles.

BREATHE DEEPLY
&
SWING ARMS FROM SIDE TO SIDE

UPPER BODY STRENGTHENING

14. & 15. Biceps Tension * with rotations

Right arm in upper curl position (boxing posture).
Left hand grips front of right wrist. Push out left arm while pulling right fist towards chin. Rotate at core from side to side slowly in a 20-degree arc, maintaining tension. Hold 3 seconds each side, for 5 full rotations.
Switch arm and repeat.

Do 1 set for each arm.

Strengthens biceps, pectoral, and shoulder muscles.

16. & 17. Triceps Pressure * with rotations

Right arm in upper curl position (boxing posture).
Left hand grips behind right wrist. Push out right arm while holding arm in place with the left hand. Maintain pressure.
Rotate at your core, from side to side. Hold 3 seconds each side, for 5 full rotations.
Switch arm and repeat.

Do 1 set for each arm.

Strengthens triceps, pectoral, and shoulder muscles.

UPPER BODY STRENGTHENING

18. Compression at Waist *
with rotations

Stand tall, place right fist in left palm.
Position hands at belly button.
Press fist into palm and maintain pressure.
Rotate at core side-to-side (20 degrees).
Make 5 full rotations.

Do 1 set.

Strengthens pectoral, shoulder, and arm muscles.

19. Tension at Waist *
with rotations

Stand tall, hook fingers together.
Position hands at belly button.
Pull hands (as if apart) and maintain tension.
Rotate at core side-to-side (45 degrees).
Make 5 full rotations.
Maintain posture!

Do 1 set.

Strengthens pectoral, arm, and wrist muscles.

UPPER BODY STRENGTHENING

20. Overhead Compression *
with rotations

Place hands high above head, right fist in palm of left hand.
Push hands together as you rotate from side-to-side.
Rotate at core for 20 degrees.
Make 5 full rotations.

Do 1 set.

Strengthens lats, pectoral, and shoulder muscles.

21. Overhead Tension *
with rotations

Place hands high above head, interlock fingers and pull apart.
Make slow side-to-side swings:
Rotate at core for a full 90 degrees to each side.
Make 5 full rotations.

Do 1 set.

Strengthens lats, pectoral, abdominal, and shoulder muscles.

UPPER BODY STRENGTHENING

22. Compression at Back
with rotations

Place hands behind back over lower spine.
Put fists of one hand in palm of other: try to push together while slowly twisting at waist.
Rotate at core side-to-side (20 degrees).
Make 5 full rotations.
Switch arm and repeat.

Do 1 set for each arm

Strengthens all back and shoulder muscles.

23. Tension at Back
with rotations

Place hands behind back over lower spine.
Interlock fingers: try to pull apart while slowly twisting at waist.
Rotate at core side-to-side (20 degrees).
Make 5 full rotations.
Switch arm and repeat.

Do 1 set for each arm

Strengthens biceps, pectoral, and shoulder muscles.

UPPER BODY STRENGTHENING

24. High Sides Compression
with rotations

Place hands on sides above waist (high).
Push in, hold, and rotate at core side-to-side for 10 degrees each side. Make 5 full rotations.

Do 1 set.

Strengthens shoulder muscles, improves posture.

25. & 26. Arms Wide Flying
with circles

Stand tall (think 'posture'), spread arms wide.
Make five foreword circles, rotating at shoulders. Breathe deeply (in through nose, out through mouth). Repeat with five backwards circles. Lower arms and shrug shoulders.

Do 1 set for each way.

Loosens shoulder joints, aids posture.

HEAD/NECK STRENGTHENING

27. Back of Neck Strengthen* *with rotations*

Place hands behind head: push gently against head.
Hold and rotate from core side-to-side (60 degree swings).
Stand tall, stomach in.
Make 5 full rotations.

Do 1 set.

Strengthens neck and loosens lower vertebrae.

28. & 29. Side of Neck Press & Hold * *left & right*

Place heel of right hand to your right temple.
Push gently for 5 seconds, with moderate pressure.
Push and hold five times, for 5 seconds on each push.
Switch arm and repeat on left temple.

Do 1 set for each arm.

Strengthens neck, face, and chin.

HEAD/NECK STRENGTHENING

30. Face Grimace
with rotations

Open mouth wide, bare teeth.
Grimace and tense face and neck.
Rotate slowly to each side while
grimacing, for five seconds on each
side.
Make five full rotations.

Do 1 set.

Firms face and neck muscles.

31. Face Lift
with rotations

Place thumbs under chin and
palms/fingers on sides of face; lift
gently while standing tall.
Rotate head to each side (10 degrees)
for 10 seconds each time.
Make five full rotations.

Do 1 set.

Strengthens face and neck muscles.

HEAD/NECK STRENGTHENING

32. Head Stretch
with grimace

Stand as tall as possible, stretch head to the sky.
Grimace and hold posture for ten seconds.
Relax and breathe deep.
Repeat five times.

Do 1 set.

Improves concentration on posture, firms face.

CORE BODY STRENGTHENING

33. Traction (standing) *
with quads press

Place hands on upper thighs;
tighten abs.
Stand as tall as possible,
then stretch up.
Press hands into thighs and rotate to
each side.
Make five full rotations maintaining
pressure.

Do 1 set.

*Strengthens lower spine, eases lower
vertebrae pressure.*

34. Pelvic Tilt (standing) *
with abs tension

Place hands low down on glutes, press
in as if to tilt pelvis.
Resist, and stand erect.
Tighten abs, maintain pressure, and
rotate slowly side-to-side.
Make five full rotations.

Do 1 set.

*Strengthens abs and arms, reduces lower
back pain.*

CORE BODY STRENGTHENING

35. Lower Back Stretch

Place hands at sides, press in.
Tighten abs and lean back carefully
just 10 degrees.
Hold arch position for five seconds.
Repeat five times.

Do 1 set.

Loosens and eases pressure on lower core.

36. Low Back Press
with abs resistance

Place hands on lower back, above
glutes; tighten abs.
Press, hold and slowly rotate left for 5
seconds, then to the right for 5
seconds.
Make five full rotations.

Do 1 set.

*Stretches back muscles, strengthens abs,
relieves lower backpressure.*

CORE BODY STRENGTHENING

37. Core Swing *
left & right

Place hands on counter top of chair
back.
Bend foreword for five seconds
(push spine out).
Swing back in for five seconds
(arch spine in at core).
Breathe deep and feel the stretch.
Make five full rotations.
Do 1 set.

Eases lower back pressure.

38. Core Lateral Bends
with abs tension

Place hands above hips on waist.
Tighten abs.
Make slow side-to-side swings at waist,
keeping abs taut.
Make five full swings for each side.

Do 1 set.

*Loosens core, strengthens abs, helps
balance.*

CORE BODY STRENGTHENING

39. Abs Crunches
standing

Place hands on lower part of stomach above groin.
Press in hard and tighten abdominals.
Bend forward 10 degrees and hold for a count of five, then straighten up.
Repeat five times, maintaining pressure on firm abs.

Do 1 set.

Strengthens abs, arms, and shoulders.

40. Abs Resistance Press *
with rotations

Place thumbs on belly button and hands over stomach.
Press into stomach hard and resist by tightening abdominals.
Maintain pressure while slowly rotating from side-to-side.
Make five full rotations.

Do 1 set.

Strengthens abs, arms, and shoulder muscles.

CORE BODY STRENGTHENING

41. Waist Press
with abs resistance

Place hands on waist, standing tall.
Press into sides hard, resist by
tightening stomach.
Rotate side-to-side 45 degrees.
Make five full rotations.

Do 1 set.

*Strengthens abs, stomach and waist,
improves posture.*

42. Lower Calf Stretch Repeat *

Hold chair back for balance.
Rise up on tiptoe,
hold for a count of five.
Repeat five times.

Do 1 set.

*Warms up lower legs again prior to
aerobic workout.*

CORE BODY STRENGTHENING

43. Squat Tension *
with rotations

Place feet shoulder width apart,
squat half way.
Place hands on upper thighs.
Rotate side-to-side,
20 degrees each way.
Make five full rotations in squat
position.

Do 1 set.

*Warms upper legs and abs prior to
aerobic workout.*

AEROBIC BODY STRENGTHENING

44. & 45. Sideways Leg Holds *
left & right

Place hands on back of chair.
Tilt slightly left putting all weight
and balance on left leg.
Raise right leg out to side and hold
for a count of five. Lower and rise
again, five times.
Switch leg and repeat.

Do 1 set for each side.

Strengthens inner thigh muscles,
improves balance.

46. & 47. Rearwards Leg Holds *
left & right

Place hands on back of chair.
Tilt forward and to the right, set
balance on right leg.
Raise left leg out to rear and hold
for five seconds.
Lower and rise again, five times.
Switch leg and repeat.

Do 1 set for each side.

Strengthens hamstrings, lower back,
abs.

AEROBIC BODY STRENGTHENING

48. Slow March *
with high leg raises

Stand tall. Begin a slow cadence march at circa one full step per second (i.e. left and right). Raise knees as high as possible. Continue, with arms gently swinging, for 50 steps.

Do 1 set.

Builds endurance, helps heart health.

May also be done in a seated position.

49. Fast March *
with medium/low steps

Stand tall. Begin a fast cadence marching-in-place at circa 2 full steps per second (i.e. left-right, left-right per second). Swing arms as in marching. Continue for 50 full steps (both feet).

Do 1 set.

Builds endurance, helps breathing, strengthens heart.

May also be done in a seated position.

AEROBIC BODY STRENGTHENING

50. Posture Control Walkabout

Establish proper posture by:

- Standing tall and upright
- Breathe normal but fully
- Shoulders back and sloping down naturally
- Chin back and head erect
- Draw stomach in half-way to spine, and tighten

Now, step forward (into a walk) in this posture—
Practice walking 25 yards.
Lengthen distance week-by-week.

Do 1 set.

Strengthens abs, arms, and shoulder muscles.

COOL DOWN

Relaxation Response *

Sit and relax.

Close eyes—Empty your mind.
Breathe normally and evenly.
Maintain position for 1 minute (or longer).

Juan at Juan's Wellness Class with two super-seniors, Paul and Robert, who have been inspired to graduate from student to instructor.

Chapter 9.

Juan's Total Wellness Sample Recipes

Section Contents and Introduction

If you enjoy being in the kitchen, selecting and preparing food, and experimenting and participating in the art of cooking, you will enjoy following some of these recipes and even adding your own "touch" to them. From these 60-odd recipes, one can easily mold variations and build another sixty or a hundred new dishes.

A few notes before starting. It is essential to have good equipment. Heavy iron pans are a must (for sautéing, searing and/or slow simmering). Three sizes are necessary, with the largest being fifteen inches in diameter. You will also need a couple of Teflon-coated frying pans. In regard to lidded pots, make sure they are good, solid brands – on the heavy side – not thin, lightweight or tinny makes.

Fresh herbs are far better than dried herbs; spend the extra money in the supermarket and go for bunches of fresh basil, oregano, rosemary, thyme, dill, tarragon and—if you like it—cilantro. If you are fortunate enough to have a small herb garden, you will likely have a lot more herbs, and you will be able to be more liberal in your use of them.

I am a user of garlic, as you'll notice in many of my recipes. Simply omit garlic if you or members of your family are averse to the reek and taste of it. I do want to stress, however, that I do not crush garlic or use minced garlic that has been marinating in oil for some time: I only dice fresh garlic in a rough-cut manner and use it seared (in a heavy pan) in minimal extra-virgin olive oil before adding it as part of any dish, and I find that this method reduces the intensity of its smell. What I've said about garlic goes for any herb or condiment listed in these recipes—if you don't like one, omit it; or substitute another. Always experiment. Feel free to change ingredients. Apply your own touches. Everyone can be an artist when it comes to cooking.

Juan and his wife Bunny preparing dinner with fresh produce from their garden.

BREAKFAST

OATMEAL WITH APPLE & FLAXSEED

Buy your oatmeal from a health food store or a market that carries several varieties, such as steel-cut Irish oatmeal, rolled oats, cold oats, quick-cooking oats. Be aware that the steel-cut Irish oats should be soaked overnight before cooking. All the other oats can be cooked quickly and easily the morning of use, requiring not more than a few minutes in a saucepan.

2 Servings

¾ cup rolled oats
1 ½ cups water

1 medium apple peeled and diced
2 Tbsp. flaxseed meal

Place oatmeal and water in a small saucepan, heat over medium flame, stirring occasionally, for 3 or 4 minutes. Serve in 2 large breakfast bowls, add diced apple and a tablespoon flaxseed to each bowl. Add skim milk or the milk you prefer (soy, rice, coconut etc).

JUAN'S SPECIAL OATMEAL MIX

I mix up a large batch of my dry ingredients sufficient for 2 people for at least a week. Instead of just plain oatmeal (which is fine by the way) I add some grits to the oats— because I love grits and it's, in fact, healthy—plus oat bran, flaxseed (not meal), and an omega 3 supplement (the one I use is called Platinum Plus).

The mix comprises 3 cups rolled oats; ½ cup grits; ½ cup oat bran; 1/2 cup flax seed; ½ cup omega 3 supplement. Store in a glass jar.

¾ cup Juan's special mix
1 ½ cups water

1 cup blueberries & raspberries
2 tsp honey

Simmer special oatmeal mix in water for 4 or 5 minutes, stirring. Serve with mixed berries in each bowl, plus 1 teaspoon honey, and skim milk to suit (or other milk or hot water). Can also add ½ banana to each bowl if desired.

BREAKFAST

BLUEBERRY BUCKWHEAT PANCAKES

It's important when using only buckwheat flour, or corn flour, to find a way to keep the pancakes (or other product/s) light, not solid and heavy. The way to do that is to separate the eggs and beat the whites stiff, folding whites into the batter last.

Serves 4 to 5

¾ cups buckwheat flour	¼ cup corn flour
¼ cup flaxseed meal	1/4 cup canola oil
1 egg yolk	2 egg whites beaten stiff
2 tsp baking powder	1 Tbsp dry yeast
½ cups non-fat yogurt	1 ½ cups skim or soy milk
1 cup blueberries	Honey or pure maple syrup

Mix all ingredients in a large bowl except the stiffly beaten egg whites. Consistency should be like thick syrup. Allow to sit for 5 minutes for yeast to work (you can activate yeast faster by adding 1/4 teaspoon vitamin C powder). Heat griddle to 365 degrees. Fold in the egg whites. Ladle on to griddle in serving spoon amounts; these are medium-size 5-inch pancakes. When bubbles appear (about 3 to 4 minutes) turn with a wide spatula. Brown other side (about 2 minutes). Should make about 15 to 16 pancakes.

Serve three griddle cakes per person with 2 tablespoons maple syrup (or honey or sugar-free syrup).

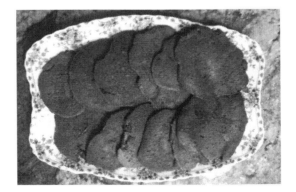

BREAKFAST

JUAN'S "BALLYCOTTON" CORNFLOUR GRIDDLE CAKES

This is a family recipe; I used to make these regularly on Sundays in the cold, often damp winters of Ireland for our 6 children. The batter makes about 50 smaller (three-and-a-half inch) griddle cakes. They are low in cholesterol and nutritious, with a lot of ingredients, so they do require more preparation time. We used to call them 'hair-on-your-chest' hot cakes. (I have modified the recipe since then, in obvious ways, i.e. less fat, less egg yolks, etc.)

1 ½ cups yellow corn flour	¾ cup buckwheat flour
¼ cup rice flour	6 tsp baking powder
½ cup rolled oats	1 Tbsp yeast (warmed/moist)
3 cups no-fat buttermilk	2 cups no-fat yogurt
2/3 cup safflower oil	3 egg whites beaten stiff
1 peeled apple diced	1 egg yolk
2 bananas mashed	½ cup chopped walnuts
½ cup oat bran	¼ skim milk as needed

Mix dry ingredients in a large bowl. Add other ingredients one at a time (except the egg whites) and stir in gently—do not beat. The batter should be thick, just loose enough to drip slowly off a serving spoon...add more skim milk if needed. Beat 3 egg whites very stiff, and fold into the batter with a few broad strokes.

Heat a large griddle to 365 degrees; lightly oil the surface with a teaspoon of canola oil (if you do not have a large griddle on your cooktop, use two heavy iron skillets, doing 3 griddle cakes per skillet at a time). The first batch may be a slightly sticky on the turn, but after that the hot cakes will turn flawlessly.

Ladle the batter on to the griddle with a serving spoon, keeping them 3 to 4 inches in diameter, no more. You should be able to cook 8 to 10 at a time. Turn them after bubbles appear on surface. Serve the hot cakes immediately while you do more batches.

Pour on a little honey, pure maple syrup, homemade black currant syrup or sugar-free syrup: Use a small bit of butter if you're dying for it, or the available non-butter butter... avoid margarine.

BREAKFAST

WHOLEGRAIN WHEAT MINI-LOAVES

These miniature "loaves" are ideal for slicing in half and eating warm with a little fat-free cream cheese and heated blueberries, or sugar-free jam, in the morning. They can be kept in a container in the refrigerator, and eaten from time to time as a snack as well (warmed in a microwave if you like) with afternoon tea.

1 ¼ cup wholegrain wheat flour	¼ cup buckwheat flour
¾ cup Juan's special oatmeal mix	2 tsp baking powder
1 Tbsp cream of tartar	1 egg yolk
2 egg whites beaten stiff	1 Tbsp dry yeast
1 tsp vitamin C powder	3 Tbsp EV olive oil
¾ cup fat-free buttermilk	1 Tbsp honey

Preheat oven to 365 degrees. Mix all ingredients in a bowl except the stiffly-beaten egg whites. Stir until consistency is like thick molasses, a medium-thick dough. After 5 minutes, fold in the beaten egg whites. Roll out the dough on a floured board, flatten to about 3/4 inch height, and divide into 20 or so circles or squares.

Place the squares on two lightly floured baking trays (and/or spray the pans very lightly with fat-free spray) and bake for 20 to 25 minutes until done. I find it best to sprinkle oatmeal mix on the trays to prevent slight burning on the bottom of the mini-loaves. Test for doneness with a toothpick, which should come out dry.

Serve with fat-free cream cheese and sugar-free jam, and/or with warmed berries.

BREAKFAST

FLAXSEED BLUEBERRY MUFFINS

This recipe makes 12 to 15 small muffins. As in the last recipe (i.e. the mini-loaves) these can be kept in the fridge for a couple of days. However, you'll probably want to give them out to your friends.

1 ½ cups whole wheat flour
½ cup flaxseed meal
3 tsp baking powder
¼ cup canola oil
3 cups blueberries
1 peeled apple chopped well
2 Tbsp honey

½ cup Juan's special oatmeal mix
¼ cup flaxseed (seed)
1 tsp bexatartar
1 ¼ cups fat-free buttermilk
1 egg (white beaten stiff)
1 Tbsp dry yeast

Preheat oven to 375 degrees. Mix all ingredients in a large bowl, folding in the canola oil and egg white last.

Spray muffin tins lightly with non-fat spray and ladle in dough to halfway mark. Allow to sit for 5 minutes. Bake for 35 to 40 minutes. Test with toothpick after 30 minutes for doneness in case oven is hotter than expected. Toothpick should remove clean and dry.

Serve muffins with coffee, herbal tea.

BREAKFAST

NO FAT GREEK YOGURT WITH RASPBERRIES & HONEY

There is not much more one can say about this breakfast dish other than it is simply delicious, filling and sustaining until the mid-morning snack. I have always preferred plain Greek Yogurt (or equally as good in the Middle East, where they call it Leban), but it seems most people prefer a flavored yogurt. If you do choose a flavored yogurt, you may not need the honey—and so save yourself a few calories, and perhaps a bit less sugar intake.

6 ounces of Greek plain yogurt   1 Tbsp local honey
½ cup red raspberries

Spoon yogurt into a soup size bowl or cereal platter, drizzle honey on top and add sweet red raspberries. You may want to take a half slice of Irish brown bread toasted, or a "mini-loaf," to round out your breakfast if really hungry.

BREAKFAST

IRISH STONEGROUND FLOUR & SODA BROWN BREAD

In the United States you can order (online or by phone) the special Irish-Style Wholemeal Flour sold by King Arthur Mills; it's a coarse, natural brown flour with husks and other grain bits un-removed—this flour makes the soda brown bread that most closely resembles the brown soda-bread in Ireland. (Or you can try to duplicate that rough flour by mixing 8 ounces of the coarsest whole wheat flour with 8 ounces of unbleached brown rice flour and throw in ¼ cup of flax seeds and ¼ cup oat bran.)

Alternatively, you can sometimes buy from a specialty Irish shop a pre-mixed flour product called Odlum's Soda Bread Mix (imported from Ireland); all one does is add water or no-fat buttermilk per instructions on the packet. We will stick with the first option above.

16 ounces Irish whole wheat flour	¼ cup flaxseed meal
¼ cup oat bran	2 Tbsp bread soda
1 ¼ cups fat-free buttermilk	1 tsp dry yeast

Mix dry ingredients in a large bowl, slowly add buttermilk while stirring and knead into a medium-thick, slightly moist dough ball. Place dough on a floured tray and flatten into a round patty about one to 1 ½-inch high: Mark a deep cross on top. Bake in a hot oven at 385 degrees for 45 minutes.
Test for doneness with toothpick, or knock on the bottom—it will sound hollow. Cool on a wire tray.

Cut slices ¾ inch thick, serve with no-sugar fruit spread or honey or marmalade and pour hot Barry's or Bewley's Irish tea from a cosy-covered teapot; or have it toasted with a good cup of real coffee in the morning. As an alternative to Barry's caffeinated Ceylon tea, try a no-caffeine tea called Rooibos from South Africa; many stores carry it now— an excellent, nutritious tea.

BREAKFAST

SCRAMBLED EGGBEATERS w CHIVES & TOMATO ROULADE

This recipe uses eggbeaters, but every once in a while we are entitled to—and can benefit from—one or two free-range chicken eggs. Be that as it may, this is a fast and simple dish and is amazingly satisfying, especially if accompanied by slices of Irish brown soda bread lightly toasted.

Serves 2

1/2 cup eggbeaters   OR 1 egg yolk + 3 egg whites
2 spring-onion diced fine   1 ounce fat-free feta cheese
1 large tomato, peeled, diced   I clove garlic, diced fine
1 Tbsp fresh oregano, chopped 1 Tbsp parsley, chopped
2 slices Irish brown soda bread   1 tsp extra virgin olive oil

Add chives and parsley to eggbeaters (or to beaten egg yolk and whites). In a hot Teflon pan with EV olive oil add garlic and oregano, sauté over medium flame for two minutes then add tomatoes that have been diced into quarter inch squares. Set aside. To hot pan, pour in beaten eggs and scramble, adding fat-free feta cheese toward the end.

Place half of scrambled eggs on each slice of toast, gently spread tomato roulade over the top, and serve.

BREAKFAST

POACHED EGG WITH VEGETARIAN HASH

I used to love to treat myself to a plate of corned beef hash with a couple of poached eggs on top and home fried potatoes, especially for a Sunday brunch meal. This is a healthy version of that dish, using portabella mushrooms as substitute for the corned beef, and sautéed zucchini slivers instead of fried potatoes. Even with only one egg instead of two, this dish is just as delicious as the original was so many years ago, and far more nutritious.

Serves 2

2 free-range-chicken eggs	4 cloves garlic, diced fine
1 medium sweet purple onion	16 ounces mushrooms
1 small zucchini, slivered lengthwise	3 Tbsp fresh oregano
¼ cup fresh parsley, diced fine	2 Tbsp EV olive oil

Dice medium portabella mushrooms and medium onion into small pieces. Sliver the zucchini into long thin strands, like macaroni. In an iron skillet, heat the EV olive oil and sauté the garlic and onion until the latter becomes translucent and fragrant. Add the mushrooms and oregano, cover and simmer for eight to ten minutes, stirring occasionally. Finally, push the mushroom hash to one side of the skillet; add parsley and the zucchini slivers to the other side and sear, covered, three more minutes.

In a separate small pan with 1½ inches of water gently boiling, carefully break the eggs into the water and poach for 3 minutes. The whites should be formed, and the yolks soft but not runny.

Scoop half of the mushroom-onion hash onto each plate; then gently lift out one poached egg at a time with a slotted serving spoon and place on top of the hash. Place half the zucchini slivers beside each hash-and-egg serving. Accompany with slices of Irish brown soda bread or with mini-loaves and sugar-free jam.

BREAKFAST

DICED FRUITS, BERRIES & NO-FAT CHEESE BUFFET

At breakfast time, whether serving at a one-on-one total immersion course, or to a group of ten (or at home alone), I would present three glass bowls and a glass dish on a buffet counter.

The three glass bowls should have fruits divided into their natural complimentary assortments, for example:

The first bowl holding a mix of red raspberries, blueberries, strawberries cut into smaller pieces, and peeled and cored kiwi fruit in circular slices:

The second bowl containing diced apple, diced pear and diced pineapple—all pieces being about one inch square, or less:

And the third bowl having whole unpeeled fruits such oranges, bunches of green and red seedless grapes, bananas and figs.

What is not consumed at breakfast can be repositioned for morning snack-time and at lunchtime: There will be little wastage, especially as our 'student/s' become used to eating far more fruits, as well as salads and vegetables, than they ever did before. After exercise class, there is nothing more satisfying than sweet fruit along with a glass of cold water.

The breakfast-time flat glass dish referred to, is for a display of fat-free cheeses such as feta cheese, goat cheese from France, cream cheese and any other no-fat cheese/s that can be found in your region, and/or from your specialty food store. Whole Foods always has an extensive selection at their cheese counters.

Serve fruit from the buffet on a medium size plate, or heap some berries and other fruit of your choice on your morning oatmeal.

BREAKFAST

COFFEES, TEAS, MILK & JUICES

One cup of real caffeinated coffee a day is okay; that's the rule of thumb for Juan's Total Wellness regimen. And if it's in the morning at breakfast time and you sneak a re-fill, well, that's all right too.

To make good coffee, always buy beans (of your choice) and grind them immediately before brewing. A good drip (filtered) or steam-pressure coffeemaker—the Italians and Germans seem to make the best—makes a big difference to the taste of the coffee.

Don't bother with the ersatz stuff: it's awful.

The same goes for tea. If you are a serious tea drinker (perhaps your mother grew up in Ireland or England, or India) you know how vital that cup of strong, real tea is first thing in the morning. If you are using a teabag, add the hot water just as or before the water begins to boil. Let it steep, stirring often; squeeze all the good stuff out of the bag with your teaspoon before you discard it.

If I am making tea for a group of, say, six or eight—or for an afternoon tea party—I will use loose tea leaves and make it in a teapot the old fashioned way: One teaspoon of tea leaves (good Ceylon tea, like Barry's from Ireland or 5 Roses from London) per cup to be poured, in the bottom of the pot. Add hot water just seconds before the boil; put the lid on, cover it with your woolen tea-cosy, and allow the tea to steep 5 minutes. For those who use milk, always add the milk to the teacup first, then pour tea into it. Don't worry about straining the leaves; they will sink to the bottom of the cup. In any event, if someone is going to read your fortune, you will want some leaves in the bottom of your cup.

In regard to milk, use skim milk in moderation. For those who are lactose intolerant, there is soy milk, rice milk, coconut milk, almond milk. As to juices, make sure they are pure fruit juices with no added sugar. Certain berry juices have been touted as merely miraculous but be careful; Do some research, read the labels, and ask your physician and/or nutritionists.

SNACK

GROUND TURKEY BREAST CHILI CON CARNE

This is as good as any Texas beef chili. Add half a cup of left over black coffee, and a tablespoon of honey, to give it extra intrigue.

Serves 6

1 ½ lb skinless ground turkey breast
5 Tbsp Laredo Texas hot chili powder
2 Tbsp rosemary chopped fine
2 Tbsp EV olive oil
½ cup left over black coffee
Dash of tobacco and soy sauces
½ cup red wine or sweet sherry
2 Tbsp chopped jalapeno peppers

6 cloves garlic, minced
¼ cup fresh oregano
1 tsp cumin powder
1 cup chicken stock
2 Tbsp local honey
(1 cup Goya black beans)
1 small apple, peeled, diced
½ tsp cayenne pepper

Brown the ground turkey meat in an iron skillet in EVOO, together with the minced garlic and chopped fresh oregano. Add chopped rosemary, apple, chili powder, cumin powder and honey together with the chicken stock. Simmer 20 minutes. Add wine or sherry, coffee, black beans (optional), jalapeno and sauces and simmer another 20 to 30 minutes, stirring occasionally. Add cayenne pepper to taste.

VEGETARIAN CHILI with WHITE BEANS (ALTERNATIVE)

This is prepared almost exactly the same way as in the recipe above. The ingredients are different of course. Add cayenne pepper and hot sauce to taste.

1 cup chopped zucchini
1 cup chopped celery
1 medium onion, diced
1 cup okra, chopped
1 cup white wine
1 tsp cumin powder
2 Tbsp jalapeno pepper
1 peeled apple, chopped
½ cup fresh herbs chopped

1 cup diced eggplant
1/2 cup chopped carrots
6 cloves garlic, minced
1/2 cup parsnip, diced
5 Tbsp Texas chili powder
2 cups vegetable stock
4 Tbsp EV olive oil
3 cups white beans
2 Tbsp local honey

SNACK

JUAN'S SPICY GAUCAMOLE & CORN CHIPS

The taste of avocado has to solidly come through in order for guacamole to be perfect. It can't be drowned out by the heat of spices, yet spices should be there—along with lemon zest and garlic, to give it body and subtlety. Add cayenne pepper to taste.

Serves 4-6

3 ripe avocado pears	3 cloves garlic, crushed
2 Tbsp EV olive oil	1 lemon, juice of and zest of peel
2 Tbsp crushed jalapeno	¼ cup finely chopped onion
½ ripe peeled tomato, crushed	3 Tbsp terragon chopped fine
3 Tbsp fresh basil, chopped	¼ tsp Tabasco sauce
1 Tbsp terragon vinegar	2 Tbsp local honey

Mash avocados with olive oil and vinegar, add crushed tomatoes (seeds removed), onion, garlic and all other ingredients and stir contents well with a fork. The guacamole should not be creamy-smooth, but slightly lumpy.

Ladle into an attractive Mexican earthenware bowl, and serve with baked no-fat corn chips to use as dipping spoons.

CHICK PEA & GARLIC HUMMUS w CORN TORTILLA

The best hummus I've had has been in the Middle East. In our supermarkets in the U.S., there are a variety of humus products on offer, with all sorts of additions and flavorings that do not necessarily enhance the humus. The best course is to buy the highest quality plain humus, and enhance it yourself with a small amount of very finely crushed garlic, some olive oil to stir in with a drop or two of white vinegar, a pinch of pepper and a dash of finely chopped dill. Ladle into a glass serving bowl.

Serve the hummus—after stirring it into a smooth paste with a swirl on top painted with EVOO—with heated soft corn tortilla pieces (or alternatively, with Middle Eastern unleavened bread).

SNACK

HEARTY VEGETABLE SOUP

This is Grandmother's ultimate staple, always available in the winter, especially when someone has a cold. It is so simple to make. All that is required is some time, in order to chop all the vegetables, and a large pot of water (or saved vegetable stock).

Serves 6

2 cups chopped cabbage	1 cup diced carrots
1 cup diced celery	1 cup coarse-chopped zucchini
1/2 cup diced eggplant	½ Bermuda onion chopped fine
2 tomatoes peeled, crushed	1 cup green peppers, chopped
2 cups cooked navy beans	1 cup beet-greens' stems, diced
4 garlic cloves, diced	1 tsp soy, Worcester & bbq sauce
¼ cup fresh basil, chopped	2 Tbsp sage powder
1 tsp cayenne pepper	2 quarts water, or stock, or mix

Simmer all chopped and diced ingredients in a large pot of water (or water & saved stock combination) for 2 hours. Add cooked beans toward the end and stir occasionally. If extra body is needed, you may add some brown rice for the last half hour, or left-over cooked yams coarsely chopped.

Serve any time, morning or afternoon. Save in a container in the fridge.

SNACK

PUREE OF SQUASH SOUP

All puree soups are hearty, whether made with the main ingredient being one or more of the various squashes, or with leeks or potatoes or asparagus—whatever. Feel free to experiment. They are fun to make and delicious to consume. (As a side note, ensure that you have good utensils and cookware—thin, tinny pots will result in burned soups.)

Serves 4-6

2 butternut squash, oven roasted	2 acorn squash, roasted
2 Tbsp EV olive oil	4 cloves garlic, crushed
3 pints vegetable stock	½ pint no-fat yogurt
1 cup fresh tarragon, finely diced	1 cup parsley, chopped
1 tsp Tabasco sauce	1 tsp white pepper
½ pint non-dairy no-fat 'creamer'	2 cups cooked yam, mashed

Cut squashes in half, brush the cleaned insides with olive oil and roast in 400 degree oven for 50 minutes. Scoop out pulp from skins and, in a large wooden bowl, mash fine with rest of the olive oil, adding pepper, Tabasco, garlic and finely diced herbs. Stir in the mashed, leftover cooked yams, and continue to beat the puree until smooth. (You can use an electric blender or mixing machine if you prefer an even creamier-smooth soup).

Transfer mixture to a large, heavy cooking pot, add the vegetable stock (if none available, use no-fat chicken stock—or as a last resort, plain water will do) and, stirring occasionally, bring the mixture to a slow simmer. Make sure you have heat absorption pad/s between the low or medium flame and the pot; if the soup scorches on the bottom, it is ruined. Simmer 15 minutes. Slowly add yogurt and the non-dairy creamer while stirring constantly, and continue to simmer another 10 minutes. (If you feel the soup needs thickening after the yogurt is stirred in, you can add three tablespoons of cornstarch to the non-dairy creamer, well stirred, before adding that last item to the soup and simmering longer.)

SNACK

CHICKEN STOCK-BASED PEA SOUP

Pea soup is essentially just another puree soup. The method of preparation is similar to the description above (for puree of squash soup). A good pea soup will sometimes have small bits of diced ham and a distinct ham-based flavor lurking in the background. We'll omit that ingredient, but the net result is just as good in my opinion.

Serves 6

1 16-ounce pkg dried split peas	1 large red onion
2 1-pint cartons fat-free chicken stock	1 whole garlic head
1 cup rosemary finely chopped	1 cup left-over coffee
1 cup parsley finely chopped	3 Tbsp dried sage
¼ cup sodium-free soy sauce	1 cup no-fat yogurt
1 cup dairy-free no-fat 'creamer'	3 Tbsp cornstarch
1 tsp cayenne pepper	2 cups cooked yams
2 Tbsp EV olive oil	

Place dried split peas (pre-rinsed) in a heavy cooking pot with the chicken stock, old coffee and herbs and bring to a boil; then simmer covered for an hour.

Meanwhile, dice the large onion and whole garlic (8 to ten cloves) very fine and sauté in an iron pan with extra virgin olive oil until the onion is translucent. After an hour add the onion and garlic to the simmering peas in stock, as well as the soy sauce and cayenne pepper, and continue cooking for another 30 minutes. Scoop the peas' mixture out with a slotted serving spoon into a separate shallow wooden bowl, and mash strenuously with a fork—or use a blender. (Leave the liquid on the cooktop in the heavy pot.) At the same time, mix cornstarch with the non-dairy creamer in small bowl and stir well. Return the mashed peas to the stock, add yogurt, mashed yams, and the dairy-free creamer/cornstarch, stirring constantly. Simmer another 30 minutes, stirring from time to time, until thick.

Serve with brown bread.

SNACK

CRUDITES & CHERRY TOMATOES w NO-FAT HERB DIP

It's not easy to select a dip flavor that is pleasing to everyone. That's why there are so many alternatives on the supermarket shelves. However, a simple herb dip made with FRESH herbs and a hint of spice, I've found to be appealing to nearly everyone, particularly if used with fresh vegetable and fruit slivers and not some artificially flavored white-flour nacho chips.

Celery, lower halves divided in 3 slivers
Zucchini cut lengthwise in long slivers
Cucumber cut in 5-inch long slivers
1 8-oz tub soft (no-fat) cream cheese
½ cup each of oregano, tarragon, chives
Juice of 1 lemon, plus 1 tsp lemon zest
1 cup cherry tomatoes

4-inch carrot slivers
4-inch apple slivers
4-inch pear slivers
4 oz no-fat sour cream
2 cloves garlic (crush)
1 Tbsp EV olive oil

Peel and prepare all the vegetable and fruit slivers. Squeeze fresh lemon juice over the apple and pear slivers. Place slivers in a 4-inch-tall glass jar with an inch of ice water in the bottom.

Empty cream cheese and sour cream into a ceramic bowl and mix together with a wooden spoon. Add all the herbs, garlic, olive oil and lemon juice and zest and continue beating all together into a smooth, herb-speckled dip.

Serve in an attractive bowl, beside the crudité, and watch it all disappear.

SNACK

BLACK BEAN & BROWN RICE SOUP

This soup is full of protein and nutrients, roughage and fiber. It has to be one of the all-time most popular soups in our southern states yet it's perfect for the colder northern climates, especially in winter.

Serves 6-8

1 16-oz package black beans	2 cups brown rice
10 cups no-fat chicken stock	1 large Bermuda onion
2 cups parsley, chopped	6 cloves garlic, minced
1 cup fresh tarragon, rosemary each	1 Tbsp cayenne pepper
¼ cup sodium-free soy sauce	½ cup medium-dry sherry

Rinse the beans and rice well. Soak the beans overnight.

Place the beans in a large iron pot with 6 cups of fat-free chicken stock and bring to the boil, adding the parsley and fresh herbs chopped fine; simmer for 2 hours. In a separate pot, cook the rice in 4 cups chicken stock—low boil for about 30 minutes—and set aside.

Sauté the onion and garlic, all diced quite small, until the onion is soft and translucent. Add the soy sauce and cayenne pepper.

Combine all in the large pot with the cooked beans, add the sherry and more stock (vegetable or chicken) if the soup appears to be too solid for your taste, and simmer very gently for another 15 minutes.

Serve hot in cup-size bowls, with warm mini-loaves on the side.

SNACK

IRISH WHOLE WHEAT SCONES
w SUGAR-FREE STRAWBERRY JAM

Although these "brown" whole meal flour scones look heavier and dryer than traditional white scones, they are not. The trick, once again, is to separate the eggs and beat the whites stiff—folding the whites into the dough batter at the very end. Also, I admit, I do use some white flour in the mix, about one-half the amount of the Irish whole meal stoneground brown flour, in order to lighten up the scones a tad for guests. I make my scones round instead of triangular, not that it makes much difference.

2 ½ cups Irish-style whole meal flour
¼ cup Juan's special oatmeal mix
2 eggs, separated, whites beaten stiff
2 tsp bread soda
1 Tbsp honey
1 ½ scant cups non-fat buttermilk

1 ½ cups white flour
4 oz non-dairy butter
1 oz dry yeast
2 tsp baking powder
1 egg whisked "egg wash"

Mix all ingredients in a bowl saving the egg whites (beaten stiff) until last. Cut the cold non-dairy butter into the flour in small pieces with a knife. Fold in the egg whites carefully. Place dough on a floured counter top, or large board, and flatten out to 1 inch high. Cut 18 to 20 rounds using the top of a tall water glass (about 2 to 2 ½ inches in diameter) and place them on two floured baking sheets. Brush the tops with the whisked egg, and bake in a hot 450-degree oven for 18 to 20 minutes.

Serve scones with a 'beginner's half-cut' made sideways through center (yielding two rounds when cut through). Show guests how to put no-fat butter, sugar-free strawberry jam, and clotted (thickened) non-fat heavy cream or sour cream on top. Have with hot Irish Barry's tea (caffeinated), or Rooibos (non-caffeine).

SNACK

GLUTEN FREE SCONES

These are a great alternative for those with sensitivities to gluten and can also be made dairy free as well. Look for a gluten-free multi purpose flour mix (such as King Arthur) in your grocery store. Xanthan gum is a natural thickener, and can be found in most local grocery stores as well—ask if you have trouble finding it. Use soy or almond milk and an alternative 'butter' to make the scones free of dairy.

1 ¾ cups Gluten-free flour blend	¾ cup currents
¼ cup honey	2 large eggs
2 tsp baking powder	1/3 cup cold milk (low-fat, soy or almond)
½ tsp xanthan gum	1 tsp vanilla extract
½ tsp salt	1 tsp cinnamon
½ stick butter or 'alternative' butter	

Preheat oven to 400 F. Grease a baking sheet or line with parchment paper. Wisk together flour blend, honey, baking powder, xanthum gum, salt, and cinnamon. Work in the cold butter till the mixture is crumbly. Stir in the currents.

Wisk together the eggs, milk, and vanilla till frothy. Add to dry ingredients, stirring until blended. The dough should be cohesive and very sticky.

Drop the dough by 1/3 cupful onto the baking sheet. Let the scones rest for 15 minutes. Brush the tops with the whisked egg, and bake for 15 to 20 minutes, until golden brown.

Serve with sugar-free jam and hot tea.

SNACK

BROWN BREAD CUCUMBER MINI-SANDWICHES

A traditional staple at English afternoon lawn-teas, cucumber sandwiches are usually served along with other small triangular sandwiches containing potted ham, soft cheese, or egg & tomato; accompanied by a gateau, and jam-roll cake slices.

Irish brown bread loaf, sliced thin	tub of non-dairy butter
2 English seedless cucumber	no fat/no-dairy mayonnaise
4 Boston bib lettuce leaves	white pepper

Remove crusts from thin-sliced Irish brown bread. Spread out on large board 12 slices of bread, two by two's. Thinly 'butter' the slices with non-dairy butter: Likewise, spread thinly a little lo-fat non-dairy mayonnaise on each slice of bread. Place a tender light-green lettuce leaf on the 6 bottom-row slices of bread.

Peel the cucumbers and slice them razor-thin with a very sharp knife. Place about 6 or so cucumber rounds on top of the lettuce on each of the bottom-row bread slices, slightly overlapping the cucumber slices. If the cucumber slices are cut VERY thin, double up with additional slices of cucumber on each bread slice. Sprinkle lightly with a pinch of white pepper.

Fold the top bread slices over to cover the bottom slices. With a sharp carving knife, cut each sandwich into four triangles. You should have 24 mini-sandwiches. There will be enough cucumber to do it again for a total of 48 mini-sandwiches.

Serve as afternoon snack, along with fruit salad, with cups of herbal and other teas.

SNACK
FAT-FREE POPCORN w OREGANO

I associate popcorn with Chicago; I don't know why, but every time I passed through O'Hare Airport for a connection (which I must have done several hundred times in my former career) I saw people munching popcorn. You can have great air-popped popcorn, without butter or salt, and it's quite filling as a snack, without many calories. Personally, I can't watch a movie without a small bag of popcorn. You can also buy bagged popcorn that is fat-free for microwave popping; there are several brands to select from.

Since we advocate drastic reduction in sodium consumption, you can try serving popcorn in a bowl with a sprinkling of dried oregano instead of salt—I find it most satisfying.

ROASTED YAM HALF w NO-FAT SOUR CREAM

Scooping out the flesh of a roast yam with a little sour cream (fat-free) dressing is delicious in the mid-afternoon break, perhaps with a cup of soup, and carries one over to suppertime.

6 raw (or pre-cooked) yams	1/2 cup fresh basil, chopped fine
1 Tbsp EV olive oil	8 oz tub no-fat sour cream
2 garlic cloves, crushed	dash Worcester sauce

If you do not have sufficient leftover yams, precook 6 washed unpeeled yams in a pot of boiling water until they are 90% done (knife slides in but still feels some firm resistance), about 25/30 minutes. Take them out and cut them in half lengthwise. Brush with olive oil, put them under broiler for ten minutes.

Serve par-roasted (seared on top) with no-fat sour cream that has been infused with basil, garlic and a dash of Worcester sauce.

SNACK

NAVY BEAN, CORN & LENTIL SALAD w GARLIC & HERBS

This salad uses mostly pre-cooked vegetables and legumes. It is nutritious and can be added to in a variety of ways; e.g. add some cooked (or raw) cauliflower and/or broccoli florets, cooked cold green beans and carrots, or halved raw cherry tomatoes.

3 cups cooked, cold navy beans	1 cup cooked corn kernels
1 cup cooked cold lentils	1 cup cooked chick peas
4 cloves garlic crushed	4 Tbsp EV olive oil
4 Tbsp red wine vinegar	2 Tbsp balsamic vinegar
2 Tbsp local honey	¼ cup mixed Italian herbs

Toss all the cold vegetables and legumes in a glass bowl. Mix separately the olive oil, vinegars, crushed garlic, honey and herbs and stir or shake well. Add to the salad and turn or fold in gently.

Serve with no-salt, no-fat corn chips, or a slice of brown bread.

LUNCH

ROAST WILD SALMON & VEGETABLES

This is THE most nutritious protein dish you can have. Wild salmon has omega-3 fatty acids that help raise HDL 'good' cholesterol—helping to protect the vascular system— and minimum to nil 'bad' oils. Vegetarians and vegans may argue with this conclusion, preferring to maintain a completely no-meat, no-fish, no-fowl policy ("nothing that walks, swims, flies or crawls") and we respect that option, but respectfully disagree in the best interests of the majority of our 75's+ population. Avoid farmed salmon.

Serves 4

1 ½ lb wild salmon fillet w/o skin
2 Tbsp EV olive oil
1 tsp fresh tarragon, chopped
½ lemon in 4 wedges
3 carrots, unpeeled, sliced
1 ½ lb fresh spinach, rinsed

2 garlic cloves, chopped
¼ fresh dill, chopped
½ lemon, peeled, slices
3 yams, peeled, sliced
1 lb de-stringed snap peas
dash white pepper

Cut skinned salmon fillet into 4 pieces. Brush salmon with 1 tsp EVOO. Sprinkle on dill, tarragon and ½ the crushed garlic. Spread half the peeled, thin lemon slices on top.

Meanwhile boil yams and carrots 15 minutes in minimal broth, mash together with 1 tsp EVOO and dash pepper. Steam the spinach and add a sprinkle of garlic and EVOO; toss and keep hot.

Sauté snap peas in large iron skillet with 1 Tbsp olive oil; set to the side. When pan is very hot and just smoking, place the salmon fillets in and sear—lemon side up— for 3 or 4 minutes. Turn and sear the other side for 3 minutes, and turn off heat: The upper sides should be nicely charred, slightly blackened. Sprinkle dill over the salmon and decorate with remaining thin peeled lemon slices and snap peas.

Serve the salmon on hot plates, arrange vegetables attractively on three sides, garnish with lemon wedges and capers. Brown and wild rice medley (cooked in broth) could accompany this meal, if a starch is desired.

LUNCH

LEMON-GARLIC PAN-SEARED CHICKEN BREAST

I demonstrated cooking this dish on ABC/Connecticut Channel-3 television. It was fast and easy since I had prepared all ingredients beforehand; I brought my own heavy iron skillet as I guessed correctly that the studio 'kitchen' wouldn't have one. The resultant thin-sliced chicken tenders were so delicious that the co-host ate most of it right out of the pan (off-camera).

Serves 4

1 ½ lbs skinless chicken breasts
2 Tbsp EV olive oil
4 cloves garlic, diced fine
1 tsp ground black pepper

1 lemon, peeled, sliced thin
½ cup fresh oregano
1 Tbsp lemon rind minced
Lemon juice from 1 lemon

Please, buy organic free-range chicken products when preparing fowl dishes, no matter what recipe. Remove all fatty pieces and sinews from the chicken breasts (skinless of course). Cut thin quarter-inch or one-third-inch slices of the breasts on the slant; each breast should yield 7 or so slices. Sprinkle ground pepper on the slices and squeeze lemon juice all over. Spread two-thirds of the very-thin lemon slices (which have been cut in half) on top of the chicken breast slices and allow to sit for a few minutes.

In a medium-hot, large (14-inch) iron pan sauté the garlic, adding finely chopped oregano after the garlic is about half-cooked. Saute, turning often, another two minutes. Push garlic/oregano to the side of pan and turn the heat up high. With pan very hot, not quite smoking, spread all the chicken slices lemon side down, and cover with the garlic-herb bits. Sear breast slices for one to two minutes (they cook through very quickly) moving them around slightly. Turn and cover them with remaining thin-sliced pieces of lemon (the remaining lemon slices have been cut in quarters). The tops of the chicken slices will be nicely browned. Continue cooking lower sides for another minute and turn heat off; test for doneness by cutting through a slice.

Serve with two green vegetables and yams.

LUNCH

PORK LOIN RAGOUT w BAKED APPLES

This recipe goes back to the early 1970s. We had it often in that decade (the seventies); my business was at that time set up and operating out of Ireland. This is a great dish for winter months anywhere.

Serves 6 to 8

2 lbs pork loin, cut in 3/4-inch cubes	1 medium red onion, diced
1 lb portabello or other mushrooms	1 red pepper, cut in strips
1 heart of celery 6 stalks, in pieces	2 tomatoes, peeled, cubed
1 carrot, peeled, in slices	4 cloves garlic, chopped
2 Tbsp fresh rosemary, diced fine	4 Tbsp fresh basil, chopped
2 Tbsp fresh oregano, chopped	1 tsp ground pepper
1 tsp paprika	I tsp ea Tabasco & soy sauce
1 tsp Worcester sauce	1 pint fat-free chicken stock
5 Tbsp EV olive oil	4 Tbsp whole wheat flour
2 cups burgundy wine (pinot noir)	

Add 2 tablespoons olive oil to a piping-hot iron skillet and sear garlic, pork loin cubes and herbs. Toss for 4 minutes, browning and sealing the meat, then add sauces. Transfer to a cassoulet-type earthenware covered baking dish. In the same hot skillet, add another tablespoon olive oil and stir-fry mushrooms, peppers, onions, celery, carrots; toss 8 minutes and add tomatoes. Transfer all to the covered baking dish.

In same hot skillet, add remaining EVOO and flour, blend and simmer 2 minutes; slowly add stock, stirring continuously. Pour this into the baking dish when thickened; add red wine and place in 400-degree oven and cook covered for 45 minutes.

Serve with a green vegetable, brown rice, and a baked apple—cored but not peeled— for each plate.

Pre-bake apples, cored, in an ovenproof dish with cinnamon, cloves and a half-glass of vermouth, for 40 minutes/380 degrees.

LUNCH

CHICKEN & TURKEY BREAST STEW

We do a lot of stews because preparation time is minimal and cooking requires no watching, and they are often quite delicious.

Serves 6

2 lb organic chicken breasts
4 yams, peeled, cut in 1" cubes
6 cloves garlic, chopped coarse
8 Tbsp extra virgin olive oil
½ cup fresh oregano, chopped
1 Tbsp freshly ground pepper
Liberal dash Tabasco sauce

1/2 lb ground turkey breast
2 Bermuda onions diced fine
2 tomatoes, peeled, chopped
4 cups cooked small white beans
1/4 cup fresh tarragon, chopped
3 cups no-fat chicken broth
3 cups peeled carrots, diced large

Cut cleaned, skinless chicken breasts into 1-inch squares and place in a large iron skillet with 6 tablespoons olive oil, garlic, onions, pepper and herbs. Cook gently over low heat until onions are translucent (about 10 minutes). Add tomatoes and yams and broth and bring to a low simmer; simmer 20 minutes. Transfer to an earthenware pot suitable for the oven.

Separately, in 2 tablespoons olive oil heated in the same skillet, sear the ground turkey breast to well done. Add Tabasco sauce and diced carrots and continue browning for 8 to 10 minutes. Add the white beans. Transfer all to the earthenware pot, stir the entire ingredients gently before placing in a 350-degree oven for 40 minutes.

Serve on warm plates with heaping chopped chard; ladle two serving spoonful's stew onto a bed of brown rice. Accompany the dish with a thick slice of Irish brown soda bread to sop up the gravy.

LUNCH

CHICKEN GUMBO w OKRA & PEPPERS

We have always loved Louisiana Creole dishes. They are like a version of paella, with almost anything to be included for a robust (or a modest) protein ingredient, but always containing a slice of spice. This gumbo is relatively mild. The okra is key; and oh so nutritious.

Serves 10 to 12

3 lb organic chicken breasts	2 lb chicken thighs (no skin)
½ lb lean white pork loin	3 Tbsp EV olive oil
6 cloves garlic, chopped coarse	1 onion, diced fine
5 peeled tomatoes, chopped	3 stalks celery, chopped
2 lbs whole okra, ends removed	2 oz whole wheat flour
¼ cup each fresh oregano, rosemary and thyme chopped fine	
¼ cup jalapeno pepper chopped	4 pints chicken or veg stock

Slice chicken and pork into 1 ½-inch strips, place in a hot iron skillet and sear all with garlic, onion and olive oil. Continue cooking until onion turns soft and transparent. Add flour and stir with a wooden spoon to make a paste; add the stock stirring continuously to thicken the sauce. Add tomatoes and celery to the pan and simmer another 30 minutes. Finally add okra and all the herbs and cover, cooking gently over very low heat for 1½ hours. This can be further thickened at the end with a 2 or 3 tablespoons of cornstarch mixed with some of the broth, stirred in gradually.

Serve with brown and wild rice—with a couple of cups of cooked chickpeas mixed in— and copious steamed fresh spinach.

LUNCH

CAJUN SHRIMP CREOLE
w ASPARAGUS & TOMATO RISOTTO

It's not really "risotto" because we use brown rice with some wild rice rather than the traditional Arborio rice, but with the way we make it, it suites perfectly being coupled with our shrimp creole.

Serves 8

FOR SHRIMP CREOLE
2 ½ lbs medium-large shrimp, peeled & deveined (about 50 to 60)
½ lb chicken breast, no-skin, cut in strips | 6 cloves garlic
1 orange pepper, chopped in 1-inch bits | 1 onion, chopped
5 tomatoes, peeled/seedless, chopped | ¼ cup tomato puree
1 cup no-fat chicken stock | 1 Tbsp jalapeno bits
1 lb fresh whole okra, ends removed | 1 cup dill, chopped
1 cup fresh parsley, chopped fine | 4 bay leaves
2 Tbsp dried oregano flakes | 1 tsp cayenne pepper
4 Tbsp EV olive oil | 3 Tbsp brown flour

FOR RICE
2 cups brown rice | 1 cup wild rice
6 cups vegetable broth | 1 tomato, peeled
½ lb cooked asparagus, cut in ½ inch bits | dash Italian herbs

Put the 3 cups rice in a large pot with 5 cups broth and Italian herbs, bring to the boil and simmer covered for 35 minutes.

Meanwhile, sauté chicken strips in 1 tablespoon olive oil in a 14-inch iron skillet, with chopped garlic, onion and cayenne pepper four 4 minutes. Add remaining 3 tablespoons olive oil and mix flour in to make a rue; gradually add broth and tomato puree stirring until thickened. Add chopped tomato, remaining herbs and okra cut into 1-inch pieces. Simmer for 25 minutes. Add shrimp in last 10 minutes only, gently stirring them into the creole mixture. Place all into a warmed serving bowl and keep hot. Turn heat under the skillet to high and transfer the nearly cooked rice into it (add 1/4 cup broth if necessary) and sear another 5 minutes with chopped tomato and asparagus, tossing to enfold.

Serve at once; ladle rice on to plates and spoon shrimp creole in centers.

LUNCH

POACHED HALIBUT w DILL SAUCE

You could use grouper or cod or any large white-flesh fish for this dish, with this recipe.

Serves 8

3 lbs fresh halibut, skinned
3 cloves garlic, crushed
2 celery stalks, chopped
3 Tbsp corn starch
liberal dash white pepper

2 pints fish stock, strained
I onion chopped fine
2 cups fresh dill, chopped fine
1 cup no-fat rice creamer
2 lemons, in quarters

Pre-make fish stock by simmering heads and fins (or other pieces of fish) in a vegetable broth with carrots and bay leaves.

Bring strained fish stock to gentle simmer in a large copper pan. Cut the cleaned fresh halibut into 8 pieces, immerse them in the stock along with chopped onion and celery. Poach uncovered for ten minutes. Remove the fish, sprinkle with 1 cup of the fine-chopped dill and set in warm oven.

Mix the cornstarch with rice creamer and stir until well absorbed. Take 2 cups of the fish stock, strained again, and in a clean pan combine the stock with the rice creamer and crushed garlic. Stir over low heat until thickened; add 1 cup chopped dill and white pepper. Continue stirring until sauce is piping hot.

Serve halibut on hot plates with dill sauce spooned over the fish and a quarter-lemon wedge aside. Accompany with boiled white and sweet potatoes, peas with pearl onions, and brown bread.

LUNCH

PAN-SEARED BLUEFISH

It is important with bluefish, or any other non-white-flesh oily fish such as mackerel or salmon, to remove the skin and any very dark (almost black) areas that are normally between the skin and the flesh. Best way to do this is to divide the skinned fillets in half lengthwise, then from the bottom up (at the divide) remove the oily dark material. The fillets should be completely clean.

Serves 6 to 8

2 large fillets bluefish (c. 3 lbs)	3 Tbsp EV olive oil
1 egg, beaten well	¼ cup whole meal flour
1/8 cup oat bran	1/8 cup flaxseed meal
2 cloves garlic, minced fine	1 cup fresh dill, chopped
1 tsp white pepper	½ cup rice milk creamer
1 lemon cut in halves for juice	2 lemons quartered

Squeeze fresh lemon juice over the bluefish fillets, cut fillets into 6 to 8 pieces and set aside. Make a thick batter in a low wide bowl by mixing flour with 1 tablespoon olive oil then adding all other ingredients. Dredge the fish pieces in the batter, turning several times.

In a large 14-inch iron skillet, heat the other 2 tablespoons olive oil to very hot. Turn exhaust fan on high as well. Lift fish fillets out of batter and place carefully in the hot pan. Turn with a spatula after 3 minutes, they will be nicely browned on top; lower the heat, cook the other sides about 5 minutes depending on thickness of the fillets (check for doneness in the middle of one fillet—it should be soft and very slightly moist, not overdone and dry).

Serve with small, peeled purple potatoes and steamed chard; place a quarter lemon on each plate. A chilled Chassagne Montrachet or Puilly Fume goes extremely well with this dish, and as a rare exception you may wish to partake of a glass at lunchtime—but, please, only once in a blue moon.

LUNCH

JUAN'S BOUILLABAISSE w STEAMED GREENS

A big dish, requiring considerable preparation time; but it's worth the effort.

Serves 8 to 10

1 lb. mussels (scrubbed, cleaned, soaked in water with vinegar)

1 lb. Gulf shrimp (peeled, deveined)	1 lb. cod (no skin, no bones)
1 lb. bluefish (skinned, cleaned well)	1 lb. wild salmon (no skin)
6 cloves garlic, chopped	1 onion chopped fine
3 tomatoes, skinned, cubed	1 Tbsp ground pepper
1 ½ cups assorted fresh herbs	1 tsp cayenne pepper
Dash Tabasco & no-salt soy sauces	3 Tbsp EV olive oil
3 cups dry white wine	¾ lb fresh whole okra
5 cups fat-free chicken broth	1 cup chopped parsley

Cut cleaned cod and bluefish fillets into 1-inch squares or cubes. Cut salmon fillet into 2-inch-long pieces. In a large covered Cruesset pot, sauté the garlic and chopped onion in EV olive oil until onion is soft. Add the 1½ cups mixed herbs (oregano, fennel, dill, turmeric, cardamom) along with ground pepper and tomatoes and heat well. Add all the fish pieces and turn gently so that all sides are heated and dredged through the garlic/herb mix. Add broth, Tabasco and soy sauces, and white wine and bring to a simmer. Add okra, mussels and parsley and simmer for 10 minutes. Finally, add shrimp, stir all ingredients gently, turn the heat off, cover and let steep for 5 more minutes.

Serve bouillabaisse in soup bowls. In a large central serving dish, have a huge mound of well-steamed collard greens (tossed beforehand with 2 tablespoons EV olive oil and 2 cloves crushed garlic) for guests to help themselves to. Offer slices of multi-grain brown bread, and a light green salad and apple slivers with drizzled honey-balsamic dressing on side plates.

LUNCH

TUNA & PRAWNS TEMPURA w RICE NOODLES

It's not possible to quite duplicate the crispy batter of golden deep-fried tempura presented in Japanese restaurants by only using a spoonful or two of oil in an iron skillet. Nevertheless, this is an attractive and nutritious, delicious dish.

Serves 6

1 ½ lb jumbo Gulf shrimp	1 ½ lb yellow-fin tuna steaks
4 Tbsp EV olive oil	1/4 cup corn flour
4 tablespoons cornstarch	3 cloves garlic minced
3 spring onions chopped fine	3 Tbsp fresh ginger root, minced
3 egg whites beaten stiff	1/8 cup no-fat chicken broth
dash cayenne pepper & turmeric	½ cup fresh parsley chopped
scant ¼ cup beer	

Cut tuna into 2-inch-long, thin strips. Peel, de-vein and rinse the jumbo shrimp (heads removed but tails left on). Prepare, in a medium size bowl, the corn flour batter adding to the flour and cornstarch the beaten egg whites, chicken broth, pepper, turmeric, parsley and the beer. Dredge the tuna strips and jumbo shrimp though the thick batter, turning often and coating all well.

In a large iron skillet, heat the olive oil with garlic, ginger and onion for a few minutes until very hot. Carefully spread the shrimp and tuna in the hot pan, turning occasionally in order to get them crispy golden all over. Turn the flame down to medium after three minutes and continue searing/sautéing for another three minutes.

Prepare brown rice noodles in a separate pot of boiling water, and snow peas in a steamer pot.

Place all (shrimp and tuna tempura, brown rice noodles and snow peas) in three attractive serving dishes and serve with a simple salad of thin-sliced peeled cucumbers and sweet onions laced with honey-balsamic vinaigrette, and green tea.

LUNCH

CURRIED PORK & SHRIMP w MANGO CHUTNEY

Curry can be mild, medium or hot. It depends on the brand and type of curry powder you get, and the extra heat you decide to add or not. I like very hot curry—my mother was born and brought up in Sri Lanka (Ceylon then) and her curries would make our heads pour with sweat. My wife likes her curry rather mild. This recipe compromises with a medium (leaning-to-mild) blend.

Serves 5/6

1 lb shrimp, peeled, deveined	½ lb white pork loin
1 medium size carrot, sliced	2 medium onions chopped
4 cloves garlic, minced fine	1 yellow pepper, chopped
2 cups vegetable broth	4 Tbsp EV olive oil
3 Tbsp whole-wheat flour	1 ½ Tbsp Madras curry powder
1 tsp turmeric, coriander & cumin	½ tsp cayenne pepper
2 Tbsp local honey	½ cup chopped fresh basil

In a large iron frying pan, sauté the pork (cut into 2-inch strips) in 2 tablespoons EV olive oil. Add carrot, chopped onion and garlic and cayenne pepper. When the meat is nicely browned, add 2 further tablespoons olive oil and stir in the whole-wheat flour and curry powder to make a rue. Add vegetable broth slowly as you stir, until thickened, and bring to a gentle simmer (use heat pad between the flame and the pan). While simmering, add all other ingredients including the peeled shrimp (tails removed as well) and allow to bubble another 6 minutes, stirring now and then.

Serve with brown rice, steamed broccoli and cauliflower florets.

To make a jar of chutney, add to a wide pot 3 peeled mangoes' flesh diced in half-inch chunks, 1 peach chopped, 1 apple chopped, 6 leechees chopped, 1 Tbsp fresh ginger diced fine, 3 Tbsp garlic crushed, 1 hot chili pepper chopped very fine (no seeds), 1 cup apple cider vinegar, 1 cup local honey, 1 Tbsp white pepper, ½ cup golden raisins, ½ cup sweet sherry. Heat and simmer 10 minutes. Cool and place in fridge to marinate for two or three days.

LUNCH

JUAN'S CASSOULET w HARICOT BEANS

This is one of my favorite dishes. It's also the only time in this list of "Juan's Wellness healthy recipes" that I introduce a meat protein other than skinless chicken breast or lean white pork meat. This exception comprises lean, all fat removed, slender, tender lamb chops. One just has to have a few lamb chops with cassoulet.

Serves 8

2 racks slender lamb chops (c. 16-20)	1 lb chicken breasts
1 lb turkey-meat Cajun sausage	1 lb haricot beans
1 large carrot diced	1 large onion diced
4 cloves garlic, chopped rough	1 orange pepper, diced
1 lb mushrooms, sliced	6 Tbsp EV olive oil
¼ cup fresh basil, chopped	2 Tbsp fresh oregano
1 Tbsp fresh basil, chopped	2 cups white wine
2 cups no-fat chicken stock	1 Tbsp paprika

Separate lamb chops and remove all fat carefully, leave on bone. Cut cleaned, skinned chicken breasts into 1½-inch strips. Cut sausage into half-inch circles. Sear all meats in a large, heavy iron skillet in which the olive oil is near smoking-hot. Toss rapidly for 5 to 8 minutes. Add the diced/chopped vegetables and mushrooms and continue cooking for 15 minutes, turning frequently.

The haricot beans should have been soaked overnight, and pre-cooked the next morning in vegetable stock for an hour with some pearl onions and whole peeled garlic cloves and set aside in preparation for addition to the cassoulet later.

To the meats, vegetables and mushrooms, add chicken stock, herbs, wine and three-quarter-cooked haricot beans. Bring back to a very low simmer and transfer to an ovenware pot; cover, and place in 300-degree oven for 1 1/2 hours.

Serve guests from the pot, along with spinach and French green beans, and slices of Irish brown soda bread.

LUNCH

WHOLE WHEAT PENNE w GROUND PORK BOLOGNESE

This is a simple and quick dish to prepare, and like almost all Italian first courses, satisfyingly delicious. You can even find dairy-free, low-fat Parmesan-type cheese to sprinkle on before serving.

Serves 2-3

1 lb ground pork loin	½ lb portabello mushrooms
3 Tbsp dried oregano leaves	4 oz lo-sodium tomato paste
8 oz crushed, peeled tomatoes	2 cups no-fat chicken stock
1/8 cup leftover coffee	2 Tbsp honey; 1 Tbsp pepper
½ Bermuda onion chopped	4 cloves garlic, minced
3 Tbsp extra virgin olive oil	

In an iron skillet, heat the olive oil; add garlic and onion, and sauté until onion is soft and translucent. Add ground pork, mushrooms and oregano, and brown the meat well. Add crushed tomatoes, tomato paste, chicken stock, coffee, honey and pepper. Stir all well and simmer gently over low heat on stovetop for an hour. In a large pot of boiling water, cook whole wheat penne for 13 to 14 minutes, drain and add a teaspoon of olive oil.

Serve penne on hot dishes, lather with Bolognese sauce and a dash of faux Parmesan cheese, along with steamed fresh spinach and sautéed zucchini.

LUNCH

CHICKEN BREAST STIR-SAUTE

Asian-type meals are excellent because one can have so many sautéed side dishes, keeping them all more or less very-low-fat, and have multiple choices to serve to guests—coupled with brown and wild rice, whole grain noodles, and/or vegetable in broth (such as Chinese cabbage or bok-choy).

Serves 6

2 lbs cleaned skinless chicken breasts	4 Tbsp EV olive oil
2 Tbsp fresh ginger, chopped fine	6 spring onions
2 cloves garlic, chopped fine	1 tsp thyme
6 Tbsp no-sodium soy sauce	6 Tbsp coconut milk
1/2 tsp Asian hot sauce or Tabasco	3 Tbsp local honey
1 cup water chestnuts, sliced	¼ cup bamboo shoots

Cut the free-range chicken breasts into 1-inch by ½-inch rectangles and sear in a hot iron pan with extra virgin olive oil for 4 minutes, tossing continuously. Lower heat to medium. Add the garlic, ginger, spring onions (cut into 2-inch pieces) and continue sautéing for ten minutes until onions and garlic are translucent and chicken is soft and tender inside. Stir in the soy sauce and coconut milk; when thickened a bit add water chestnuts, bamboo shoots, honey and hot sauce, bring all back up to high heat and toss frequently.

LUNCH

PORK LOIN w GRAPES & RATATOUILLE

It's helpful to use a meat thermometer is testing the pork loin for doneness, since if it gets overcooked it becomes very dry. It should be moist and tender on carving.

Serves 8

2 ½ to 3 lb lean pork loin	1 lb red seedless grapes
3 cups Madeira sweet wine	3 Tbsp local honey
1 tsp cayenne pepper	1 cup fresh oregano chopped
juice from 1 lemon	6 cloves garlic, minced
1 Bermuda sweet onion	6 Tbsp EV olive oil
1 tsp tarragon	dash Worcester & soy sauces

Place pork loin (trimmed of all fat) in a metal bowl and cover with Madeira wine (or other sweet red wine), add honey, half of the minced garlic, oregano, pepper, and the juice of 1 lemon. Place in refrigerator and let sit 4 hours, turning the meat once. Save marinade and transfer pork loin to a hot 14-inch iron pan in which the rest of the garlic and onion has been cooked in 3 Tbsp olive oil. Add the tarragon and liberal dashes of Worcester and soy sauces, and turn the pork loin until nicely browned all over, about 10 minutes.

Cut all grapes in half except for 10, add all to the pan along with the saved marinade except 1 cup, and bring juices to a simmer. Remove from stovetop, place in a 350-degree oven for 40 minutes. Check for doneness in center of pork with thermometer.

For ratatouille, take 5 narrow eggplant and 5 small zucchini, wash but do not peel, cut into ¾-inch rings. Place in a wide pot with remaining olive oil, with a tablespoon of dried mixed Italian herbs, and cook over high heat tossing often for 10 minutes. Cut two tomatoes into cubes and add to the pot along with a yellow pepper cut in strips and 2 or 3 spring onions chopped rough, and 1 cup of the marinade. Simmer gently for 20 minutes. All should be ready at the same time. Carve pork loin on a platter in half-inch wide slices, with hot grapes surrounding, and juices from meat pan in a sauce dish.

Serve with the ratatouille, and brown and wild rice mixed.

LUNCH

CHICKEN CURRY w BROWN BASMATI RICE

You may not be able to find brown basmati rice, so fake it by mixing a third basmati with a third brown rice and a third wild rice. Cook the wild and brown rice separately since these two take considerably longer than basmati; mix together in the last ten minutes and finish off by 'steaming' the three mixed rice/s in a hot 400-degree oven.

Serves 6

2 lbs chicken breasts, skinless	8 Tbsp EV olive oil
4 garlic cloves, sliced rough	1 red onion, sliced rough
4 Tbsp Madras curry powder	1 tsp cardamom
1 Tbsp thyme	1 apple, peeled, chopped
1 mango, flesh diced	2 cups fat-free stock
2 Tbsp cornstarch	¼ cup coconut milk
2 Tbsp golden raisins	1 plantain, in 1-inch slices

Cut chicken breasts into 1-inch cubes, sear in a big iron skillet with 6 tablespoons olive oil, garlic, onions, thyme for 10 minutes tossing often. Add the curry powder, cardamom, apple, mango, and raisins; stir all together for a few minutes and pour in the fat-free chicken stock. Simmer for 10 minutes. Mix cornstarch with the coconut milk until well absorbed, then pour into the hot skillet while stirring to thicken the liquid. Add the plantain at the last and continue simmering gently for 10 minutes.

Cook the rice in two separate pots, the mixed brown and wild rice for 10 to 15 minutes longer than the basmati rice. Add 1 Tbsp olive oil to each pot as the rice/s are cooking.

Serve this dish with carrots and a green vegetable. Have three or four small bowls with condiments and surprises to sprinkle on the curry that's ladled over rice: i.e. fresh coconut slivers, dried cranberries, small diced pieces of bananas preserved from browning with lemon juice, slivers of candied ginger, chutneys.

LUNCH

VEGETABLE CURRY
w CAULIFLOWER, YAMS, ZUCHINNI & TOMATO

This is a good vegetarian lunch for those who enjoy curries, and a change from the Western consumer's almost daily reliance on a portion of meat or fish protein. Nearly all Indian, Sri Lankan or Pakistani curries are accompanied by white rice. Instead, try to have brown rice or a mix of unbleached unprocessed rice options; they are more filling with smaller amounts (thus less calories), have more fiber and are far more nutritious overall.

Serves 4 – 6

1 cauliflower, washed, in 8 wedges	5 small zucchini, sliced
2 large tomatoes, peeled, cubed	3 cooked yams, peeled
4 cups vegetable stock	4 Tbsp EV olive oil
5 Tbsp Indian curry powder	3 tbsp cornstarch
1 cup coconut milk	1 Tbsp paprika
3 Tbsp local honey	1 cup fresh pineapple diced
3 cloves garlic chopped	1 sweet onion, chopped

Heat garlic and onion in olive oil in a large pot, stirring until the onion is soft and light brown. Add zucchini slices (1-inch thick) and toss for further 5 minutes, then add curry powder and paprika, continuing to stir for a few minutes. Mix cornstarch in the coconut milk until absorbed; add this and the vegetable stock, plus tomatoes, to the pot. Stir and allow the thickened liquid to come to a gentle boil. Add the cauliflower and let simmer for 20 minutes. Add diced pineapple chunks and pre-cooked yams (cut into similar sized cubes) to the curry for the final five minutes. If necessary to thicken further, stir in a teaspoon cornstarch blended in rice milk.

Remove to a heated serving dish. Ladle on to luncheon plates over rings of brown or wild rice, with steamed carrots and braised celery on the side. Accompany with hot Ceylon tea and lemon, and soft wholegrain near-Eastern bread or yellow corn tortilla.

LUNCH

VEGETABLE & SOY CHILI w BROWN RICE & BLACK BEANS

Here's another great vegetarian lunch dish, perfect if made spicy-hot for winters in the northeast (or made milder and sweeter for y'all in the south and west).

Serves 4

3/4 lb. solid soy bean curd	1 medium zucchini, diced
1 carrot, peeled & diced	1 medium onion, diced
4 cloves garlic, minced	3 stalks celery, diced
2 tomatoes, peeled & crushed	1 cup dates, diced fine
½ cup left-over coffee	3 Tbsp Texas chili powder
1 Tbsp jalapeno minced	Pinch cayenne pepper
¼ cup fresh oregano	2 cups vegetable stock
1 ½ cup brown rice, washed	8-oz low-sodium black beans
3 Tbsp EV olive oil	1 tsp coriander & sage each

Sauté garlic and onion in a large iron skillet in extra virgin olive oil until the onion is soft and translucent. Set aside. Turn up heat, and in the hot oily pan sear the soy bean curd that has been cut into small 1/2-inch squares, tossing frequently, until they are nicely brown all over. Set aside with the garlic and onion. Add the diced vegetables with the chili powder and sauté in the hot pan until done (about 12 minutes) then pour in the vegetable stock, along with the coffee, tomatoes and dates. Simmer for 15 minutes, adding all herbs and peppers, reducing the liquid by one half. Return the garlic, onion and bean curd to the pan mixture and stir in gently over medium heat until piping hot.

During preparation of the chili (which should take no more than 45/50 minutes), you will have cooked the brown rice in 3 cups of water (or in broth if you prefer). Simmer the rice—tightly covered—for 30 minutes, then stir in the cooked black beans, cover and cook gently for another 10 minutes. Turn off heat, uncover, and allow rice and beans to sit for another 5 minutes.

Serve immediately with a green vegetable, like broccoli or kale.

LUNCH

TUNA w SHITAKE MUSHROOMS & WATER CHESTNUTS

You can of course use wild king salmon instead of tuna, or any other large fish such as halibut or cod (but avoid shark meat).

Serves 4

1 ½ lb. cleaned fresh tuna	1 can water chestnuts, rinsed
1/2 lb. young, stringed snap peas	¼ cup bamboo shoots, rinsed
1 lb. shitake mushrooms	2 Tbsp sodium-free soy sauce
1 tsp Worcester sauce	dash cayenne pepper
1 Tbsp fresh rosemary	4 cloves garlic, minced
2 Tbsp EV olive oil	1 medium sweet onion, diced
1 cup hot chicken broth	

In a hot iron skillet, sauté the mushrooms, onion and garlic in olive oil until the diced onion is just becoming translucent, then add the snap peas and toss vigorously for three or four minutes. Add the water chestnuts and bamboo shoots, herbs, pepper and soy and Worcester sauces and continue to sear for another two minutes.

Transfer contents of skillet to a ceramic baking dish and place in a warm oven (at 250 degrees F). Return the very hot skillet to the cooktop flame and carefully lay in the cleaned fresh tuna steaks (all dark bits removed) that have been cut into 4 pieces. The tuna steaks should be about an inch and a quarter thick. Sprinkle with another dash of sodium-free soy sauce. Do not sear more than a minute each side. Remove the steaks and add them to the baking dish in the oven (to sit on top of the pre-cooked shitake mushroom mixture) then pour over the cup of hot fat-free chicken broth, and allow all to remain in 250-degree oven for fifteen minutes.

Serve with brown rice (cooked in vegetable broth with a dash of paprika), and roasted celery or braised cabbage or other fiber-rich vegetable of your choice.

LUNCH

MUSSELS IN SHERRY BROTH w GARLIC & ROSEMARY

This is a simple dish but definitely tricky to get the taste just right. The broth should not be insipid, nor should it be overpowering—drowning out the taste of fresh mussels and the sea. I use fat-free chicken broth (instead of vegetable or fish broth) as a base, with a modest amount of a good dry sherry added to it. In a Dublin or Paris restaurant, they might serve mussels with a large plate of french-fries on the side. I substitute pre-cooked potato slices scorched in a hot, heavy pan with just a teaspoon of olive oil until brown and crispy and even more delicious than pomme-fritte.

Serves 2

2 pounds fresh mussels in shells	1/2 cup white vinegar
5 cloves garlic, minced	8 spring onions, cut fine
¼ cup fresh oregano, chopped	1/4 cup fresh rosemary
½ cup fresh parsley, chopped	3 Tbsp EV olive oil
2 pints fat-free chicken broth	1 cup medium-dry sherry
1 Tbsp white pepper	1 tsp Worcester sauce
Dash Tabasco sauce	2 Tbsp local honey

Scrub mussels in cold water so that all hair is removed from shells and rinse well. Place mussels in a large basin of cold water and add half the vinegar; allow mussels to soak for 30 minutes. In a large heavy pot, sauté minced garlic and spring onions in olive oil with all the herbs until the garlic is cooked but not burnt. Add pepper, Tabasco and Worcester sauces, and toss for another minute. Separately, heat the chicken broth to simmering. Pour the chicken broth into the large pot, add the medium-dry sherry and honey, and bring back to simmering. Allow the broth and contents to simmer for 20 minutes, stirring occasionally; add the drained mussels and rest of vinegar, cover, turn up heat and simmer another five to seven minutes. Stir and make sure all mussels have opened. Discard any mussels that remain closed.

Serve up in two big serving bowls, another central bowl for empty shells, with individual soup bowls and side dishes for potatoes and asparagus.

LUNCH

BROWN PASTA
w CHERRY TOMATOES, OLIVES, OKRA & NUTS

This is a variation on "Pasta Putanesca" (which is also delicious, but what with anchovies and capers, a little strong for most tastes). For those that don't like okra, just leave it out; or substitute some other vegetable such as small broccoli florets.

Serves 4 to 6

16 oz. pkg. whole-wheat penne pasta
1 cup whole black olives, pitted
1 cup pine nuts (or walnuts)
4 Tbsp EV olive oil
1/2 tsp black pepper

3 cups cherry tomatoes
½ lb. whole okra
4 cloves garlic, chopped
1 cup fresh oregano
1 cup fat-free chicken broth

Cook whole-wheat penne in a large pot with 2 quarts boiling water, about 13 minutes, with a drop or two of olive oil in the water.

Separately, sauté the garlic in a large iron skillet with the olive oil. Gradually add the oregano and nuts and stir with the garlic. Add chicken broth, tomatoes, olives and pepper and simmer all over medium-high heat for five or six minutes. Cut the stem ends off the okra, and snip the tips of the other ends, and add them to the broth mixture, stirring and simmering another five minutes.

Drain the penne pasta, place in a 15-inch-diameter serving dish, and pour the tomatoes and okra mixture all over.

Serve piping hot on warm plates, with optional grated fat-free cheese, and slivered French green beans. Use Irish brown soda bread for mopping up.

DINNER

MEXICAN TAMALE PIE w CHILI SAUCE

This is not a true "Mexican" dish, but it does approximate the delicious taste of tamales and is easier to make and serve to a group of people. The chili sauce can be either "quite spicy" or "fairly mild," depending on your guests' preferences.

Serves 8-10

2 lbs. ground turkey breast	1 large onion, diced fine
8 cloves garlic, minced	1/2 jalapeno pepper, minced
1 tsp cumin powder	6 Tbsp EV olive oil
1 cup fresh basil, chopped	½ cup fat-free chicken broth
2 tsp ground peppercorns	2 Tbsp chili powder
4 cups vegetable broth	1 6-oz can tomato paste
2 Tbsp cornstarch	6 Tbsp chili powder
4 Tbsp local honey	½ cup left-over black coffee
Dash white pepper	Tabasco Sauce to suit taste
2 doz. yellow corn tortillas	2 tsp EV olive oil

In a double boiler, steam the tortillas so that they are warm and pliable but do not break apart when handled. For the sauce: Stir a little cold broth into a glass with the cornstarch and set aside. Heat the 4 cups vegetable broth and coffee, stir in the tomato paste and chili powder, and allow it all to simmer for a few minutes. Add pepper and Tabasco; slowly add the glass of broth with cornstarch, stirring while the sauce thickens. Set aside.

For the filling: In a heavy skillet with EV olive oil, sauté the ground turkey well, and all other ingredients listed with the half cup broth and allow to cook a further fifteen minutes. Now, in a lightly oiled, large (14-inch) square, ceramic dish (2-inch deep), place a cupful of sauce in the bottom and line it with 9 -10 steamed, open tortillas allowing them to curve up and cover the sides of the dish. Fill the dish with the ground turkey mixture. Cover all with the rest of the tortillas and pour remaining sauce on top. Bake in a 350-degree oven for 40 minutes.

Allow pie to cool 10 minutes before serving.

DINNER

SKINLESS DUCK BREAST & PORK PATE
w IRISH BROWN TOAST

This pate should be served cold with a simple side salad of tomato wedges, cucumber slices and Boston bib lettuce (and a plum and cherry Cumberland hard sauce for the pate); with a bowl of hearty soup accompanied by toasted Irish brown soda bread and hot tea.

Serves 6 - 8

2 skinless duck breasts	2 slices white pork loin
4 Tbsp EV olive oil	4 Tbsp non-dairy faux 'butter'
2 Tbsp oregano flakes	2 Tbsp thyme powder
1 1/4 cups fat-free chicken broth	4 garlic cloves, crushed
2 tsp crushed peppercorns	2 Tbsp arrowroot
1 tsp Worcester Sauce	Dash Tabasco Sauce

Clean the duck breasts and pork loin, cut into thin slices, cover in a small pot and simmer in 1 cup of chicken broth with oregano until the meats are done medium-well (circa 15 minutes). Remove to a cutting board and chop the duck and pork into a coarse mince, saving any broth left in the pot.

Stir arrowroot into a quarter cup of cold broth and keep aside. Place the minced meats in a glass or ceramic bowl together with the crushed raw garlic, thyme and pepper, and gradually stir in the EV olive oil and non-dairy 'butter.' When thoroughly mixed, slowly blend in the 1/4 cup broth with arrowroot, together with any of the broth left over from simmering the meats. Add Tabasco and Worcester sauces. Pack the mixture in a six-inch-diameter/five-inch-high tureen, add 2 tablespoons of Irish whiskey to the top, and place in a 300-degree oven for 2 hours. Remove, allow the tureen to cool, and keep it overnight and a day in the refrigerator.

Serve from the tureen with an ice-cream scoop or large desert spoon, placing two scoops per salad plate. Toast 12-14 slices of Irish brown yeast bread under the broiler and cut into 24 or more 2-inch-wide wedges. Present a cut-glass bowl with deep-red Cumberland sauce to pass around, and a separate small bowl with hot Coleman's English mustard (or the milder Grey Poupon).

DINNER

TOMATO, MUSHROOM & GARLIC PIZZA

Making pizza pasta and crust without white flour is not as simple as one might expect. Nevertheless, using whole grain flour and a few tricks to lighten the brown dough, one can get close to the real thing. This is a hearty pizza, and makes one think of Naples.

Serves 6 – 8

1 lb. Irish wholemeal flour	6 Tbsp EV olive oil
¼ lb. corn flour	½ cup cornstarch
1 oz. dried yeast	1 ½ cups warm water
1 tsp Vit.C powder	1 tsp garlic powder
1 15 oz. can peeled tomatoes	¼ cup tomato paste
½ lb. portabella mushrooms	3 Tbsp fresh oregano, chopped
3 cloves garlic, diced	1 egg white beaten stiff

Mix the cornstarch and corn and wholemeal flours in a large bowl, then gradually pour the warm water (with yeast dissolved) into the flour while stirring. Add 2 tablespoons of olive oil and the garlic powder and begin kneading the dough, forming it into a ball and working the beaten egg white into the dough at the end. Use a little extra flour to prevent sticking. Cover and set aside for the dough to rise in a sunny spot or warm oven for two hours.

In a heavy skillet, sauté slivered mushrooms and diced garlic, along with fresh oregano, in 4 tablespoons olive oil until nicely done. Stir in the tomato paste, mixing well with the pan's residual oil. Cut the whole peeled tomatoes into quarter-inch slices. Roll out dough on a floured board or counter-top, to less than a quarter-inch thick, and cut it into 6 or 8 squares. Paint onto each square the tomato paste/mushroom mixture. Spread tomato slices on top of each square, sprinkle with a little fresh oregano, and squirt with a quick spray of Pam-olive-oil. Place the squares on two baking sheets and place in very hot oven (470 degrees F) for 15 minutes. As a variation you can make this into 'pizza putanesca' by adding a few capers, well-rinsed anchovies and sliced black olives on top of the tomato slices before placing squares in the hot oven.

DINNER

JUAN'S FISH STEW over BROWN RICE w CHARD

You can use all sorts of variations of this recipe, changing the selection of seafood and shellfish, or the broth and/or vegetables. It is always good.

Serves 6

½ lb. skinned, clean monkfish
½ lb. skinned halibut
4 peeled medium tomatoes
2 stalks celery in 1-inch pieces
1 onion, diced
1 pint fat-free chicken broth
1 tsp Worcester Sauce
1 cup dry white wine

½ lb. skinned wild salmon
1 lb. deveined U.S. gulf shrimp
½ lb. whole okra, de-stemmed
2 peeled carrots, in ½-inch rings
3 cloves garlic, diced
2 cups fresh dill chopped fine
1 tsp white pepper
¼ cup medium sherry

Cut all the washed fish into roughly 1-inch squares and place in a large rectangular LeCrusette iron pan. Add the peeled, deveined shrimp (tails removed). Sauté the onion and garlic, celery and carrots in a separate pan over high heat for 5 minutes, turning frequently. Add this mixture and all remaining ingredients to the pan with the fish and place in a 375-degree oven for half an hour.

Serve over cooked brown rice, with heaping steamed chard on the side.

DINNER

SWEET & SOUR FISH CUBES w ACORN SQUASH

As a reminder, suppers (or dinners) are supposed to be lighter than main-meal luncheons. So the evening portions should be smaller. And the overall calorie content should be less. In many of the supper recipes listed herein, I have included proteins— yes, including meat or fish protein—but the intention is to have these protein element/s serve as moderate supplements to vegetable, salads' and carb's lower-calorie-density portions on your plates.

Servings 4

½ lb. wild coho salmon, skinned
1 garlic clove, crushed
1 tsp black pepper
2 Tbsp EV olive oil
2 Tbsp white balsamic vinegar
3 Tbsp local honey
1 Tbsp tomato paste
1 Tbsp corn flour

½ lb. sashimi grade tuna
1 oz. fresh ginger, diced
1 tsp wasabi paste

2 Tbsp lemon juice
2 Tbsp no-salt soy sauce
1 Tbsp cornstarch
1 Tbsp Thai hot sauce

Make the sweet and sour basting sauce first by mixing together the vinegar, lemon juice, soy sauce, tomato paste and honey. After blending well, stir in the cornstarch, corn flour and hot sauce.

Cut the fish into 1-inch squares or cubes. Rub them in the crushed garlic, diced ginger, wasabi paste and pepper. Heat the olive oil in an iron skillet until it is almost smoking, then sear the fish cubes quickly, turning them often, until they are nearly cooked through.

For the final two minutes, add the sweet and sour sauce to the hot pan and toss the fish cubes frequently. Remove and serve at once with pre-cooked acorn squash, re-fried wild rice with raisins, and steamed spinach.

DINNER

SHRIMP & SQUID 'NASI GORENG' w VEGETABLE PLATE

This is essentially a re-fried brown rice dish with tasty tidbits of seafood or meat protein added, as well as flavor enhancers like onion, garlic, nuts, herbs and Asian spices.

Serves 8

12 cups pre-cooked brown rice	1 lb. deveined peeled shrimp
1 lb. cleaned calamari rings	1 large sweet onion, diced
6 cloves garlic, diced fine	1 Tbsp ground black pepper
8 Tbsp EV olive oil	1 tsp curry powder
2 tsp medium chili powder	3 Tbsp coriander
3 Tbsp salt-free soy sauce	4 Tbsp local honey

Chop the cleaned shrimp and calamari rings into small quarter-inch size bits and cubes. If you do not already have a refrigerated container of left-over cooked brown rice from an earlier meal, cook enough brown rice in a pot of water to yield 12 cups of cooked rice: Set aside the rice in a warm oven.

In a large iron skillet, sauté the onion, garlic and chopped calamari rings in 4 tablespoons of extra virgin olive oil, until the onion is translucent. Add curry powder, chili powder, pepper and coriander and toss for a few minutes. Turn the heat up very high and add the diced shrimp and cooked rice to the pan along with the remaining 4 tablespoons olive oil, soy sauce and honey. Toss vigorously for another seven or eight minutes, until the whole fried rice mixture is thoroughly heated throughout.

Serve with an assortment of oven-roasted vegetables (for example, zucchini rings, red and green pepper slices, mushrooms, celery stalks, endive hearts, eggplant slivers).

DINNER

CHICKEN SATAY SKEWERS
w CHUTNEY & CHINESE CABBAGE

The reason we have so many Asian-oriented dishes is that they are relatively easy to prepare, are delicious, are often minimal in animal or fish protein amounts and can be surrounded by wide varieties of vegetables. I travelled and worked in the East a great deal during my consulting career, and not only collected recipes in those nations but experimented back home with adaptations.

Serves 6

1 ½ lbs. no-skin chicken breasts
1 cups coconut milk
1 Tbsp ginger powder
1 tsp turmeric
3 Tbsp EV olive oil
2 Tbsp cornstarch

2 Tbsp no-salt soy sauce
¼ cup local honey
3 cloves garlic, crushed
1 tsp coriander
1 tsp cayenne pepper
1 cup fat-free chicken broth

Cut chicken breasts into 1-inch cubes, and sear in a hot iron pan in olive oil and garlic for one or two minutes. Remove chicken and set aside to cool. In a ceramic bowl, stir cornstarch gradually into the chicken broth, then add the coconut milk, ginger and other spices, and the honey and pepper. Stir all well. Add this liquid to the cooling iron pan and continue to stir as it thickens somewhat. After 3 or 4 minutes, pour all the liquid and garlic bits back into the bowl and add the chicken cubes to marinate (best to marinate for a few hours in a fridge if time permits).

When ready to grill, spear the chicken cubes onto 6 metal skewers. Place the skewers on a baking sheet and place close under an oven grill, turning them every minute and carefully dribbling on or painting some of the marinade left in the bowl. Continue to grill until chicken is nicely brown all over and cooked through, about ten minutes.

Remove and place the skewers on a large flat serving dish accompanied by Chinese cabbage that has been braised in stock, roasted carrots glazed with the same marinade, and a large bowl of Indian apple/mango chutney.

DINNER

COCONUT-SEARED TOFU w GARLIC FRIED WILD RICE

Soy in moderation is fine. Consuming too much soy on a daily basis is not considered to be in your health's interest. If you are lactose intolerant, it's often recommended that you drink rice or hemp milk instead of soymilk. However, occasional use of tofu (bean curd) in main dishes is a sensible alternative to meat protein.

Serves 4

1 lb. block solid fresh tofu	4 Tbsp EV olive oil
6 cloves garlic, minced	4 Tbsp shredded coconut
1 cup coconut milk	1 tsp hot chili powder
1 Tbsp Hoisin sauce	¼ cup bamboo shoot, sliced
6 cups cooked wild rice	4 spring onion tops, chopped
1 tsp black pepper	pinch thyme and coriander

Cook enough wild rice (about 2 cups) in gently boiling water for 40 minutes, to make 6 cups cooked rice: Set aside. Cut the fresh bean curd into ¾-inch cubes and place in a bowl with the Hoisin sauce, half the coconut milk, thyme and coriander. Allow the tofu to sit aside while cooking the rice.

In a large iron skillet, sauté a quarter of the minced garlic for three minutes in 2 tablespoons hot olive oil, add the rest of the coconut milk and stir in the shredded coconut, bamboo shoot and chili powder. When well mixed, add the tofu and liquid contents of the bowl into the hot pan and continue to stir gently, occasionally turning the tofu with a spatula until brown all over. Place in an oven-proof serving dish and remove to the oven at 250 degrees.

In the same hot skillet, add the rest of the oil and garlic and cook over high heat for 2 minutes. Add the six cups of cooked wild rice and toss vigorously for six or seven minutes, sprinkle pepper on top and add the chopped green spring onion tops for decoration.

Serve the coconut-seared tofu on top of the wild rice with heaping steamed kale on the side, and a green salad with cherry tomatoes.

DINNER

CHICKEN & PORK DUMPLINGS w BROWN NOODLES

Asian dumplings make for a nice light supper—it's almost like a hors d'oeuvres dish—so it can be accompanied by large bowls of hearty soup.

Serves 6 – 8

½ lb. skinless chicken breast
2 cloves garlic, minced
1 Tbsp no-salt soy sauce
1 tsp white pepper
½ lb. whole wheat flour
1 egg white, beaten

½ lb. white pork loin
2 spring onions, chopped
4 Tbsp EV olive oil
2 Tbsp Hoisin sauce
3 Tbsp cornstarch
1 cup hot water

Make a soft dough from the whole wheat flour, cornstarch and egg white by adding the hot water gradually while stirring. Knead the dough and roll it out on a floured counter top to less than a quarter inch thickness. Using the top of a water glass, cut out circles (the flattened dough should yield between 20 and 30 rounds).

Mince the chicken breast and pork loin into tiny pieces and place them in a mixing bowl. In a hot iron skillet with EV olive oil, sauté the garlic and minced meats, add the chopped spring onions, soy sauce and Hoisin sauce and a teaspoon of white pepper. Toss until well done and meats are browned.

In the center of each dough circle place a spoonful of the minced meats. Fold the edges of the circle up into dumplings, and press the edges closed with fingers (wet the fingers to moisten the dough edges). Place all the dumplings in one or two steam boilers and steam for twelve to fifteen minutes (use the longer time if all dumplings are in one steamer).

Serve with plum sauce and hot spicy mustard sauce, three or four dumplings per person.

DINNER

PORK LOIN w PEANUT SAUCE & ROASTED APPLE

This is perhaps the simplest of all dishes in this section of sample recipes. The roast looks after itself in the oven. The peanut sauce takes no more than a few minutes to make. And the roasted apples require just cutting in half and a bit of trimming.

Serves 10

3 lb. trimmed pork loin roast	1 Tbsp fresh oregano, chopped
6 garlic cloves, crushed	1 lemon, cut in halves & 2 slices
1/2 cup unsalted peanuts	4 Tbsp EV olive oil
1 Tbsp chili powder	1 tsp curry powder
1 tsp coriander, ground	1 tsp ginger powder
1/4 cup local honey	1 Tbsp Hoisin sauce
½ cup white balsamic vinegar	1 Tbsp peanut butter
5 crisp red apples, halved/cored	40 cloves & 10 pinch cinnamon

Brush the pork loin with olive oil, sprinkle oregano on top with two slices of lemon, place in the oven on a rack in a pan, at 400 degrees for 40 minutes or to an internal temperature of 170 degrees.

Grind ½ cup unsalted peanuts in a coffee grinder and place in a small mixing bowl. Add the olive oil, garlic, chili and curry powders, the ginger and coriander, plus the honey and Hoisin sauce and stir all together well. Add the balsamic vinegar and peanut butter, and squeeze in juice from the two lemon halves.

Peel and cut the apples in half, remove cores, stick 4 cloves on top and a sprinkle of cinnamon; place them on a baking tray and brush with a little peanut sauce. Roast them in the 400-degree oven along with the pork roast for the last 20 minutes, then (after removing the pork roast for carving) finish the apples off under the broiler for 7 or 8 minutes until tops are just scorched.

Serve each person two thin slices of pork roast with peanut sauce to the side, and a roast apple-half; plus boiled yams and French slivered green beans to accompany (and a glass of claret).

DINNER

POACHED EGG on IRISH BROWN TOAST w "FRIES"

Sometimes there nothing like 'breakfast food' in the early evening, along with hot tea and preserves, especially in the winter. When I was young we used to have poached eggs on top of Welsh Rarebit (lots of melted cheese and butter and mustard), and more sides of toast with gobs of butter and gooseberry jam. We don't do that today, but the memories linger on.

Serves 4

4 slices Irish brown soda bread	4 large free-range eggs
4 Tbsp sugar-free cherry preserves	pinch white pepper
4 peeled cooked potatoes, sliced	1 Tbsp EV olive oil
1 tsp Italian mixed dried herbs	½ tsp garlic powder

Take 4 left-over boiled potatoes, peel and slice them into quarter-inch slices. Sprinkle on dried Italian herbs and garlic powder, and sear in a very hot iron skillet with 1 tablespoon of olive oil. Turn the potatoes now and then until crispy and brown all over.

Meanwhile, poach the four eggs in gently simmering water until the whites are solid white, the yolks are still soft but not runny (about 3 minutes). Remove with a slotted spoon and place each on top of a slice of Irish brown bread toasted.

Serve immediately with a heap of sautéed potatoes and a dollop of cherry preserves on the plate, with an extra half-slice of toast on the side, and hot tea.

DINNER

ROAST MONKFISH w BROWN SAUCE & GARLIC

Monkfish (called angler fish in England or "boiderie" in Provence) is simply the most delicious seafood, if prepared properly, because (a) it has a marvelous firm texture, something like succulent young game fowl; (b) it takes on some of the taste of the sauces and spices it is paired with by a good chef; and (c) despite its "before-being-cleaned-ugliness," it is elegant when prepared for cooking, and it is healthy, that is, free of bad fats and oils.

Serves 6

2 lb. cleaned, skinned monkfish	1 lemon, halved, & 2 slices
2 cloves garlic, minced fine	2 cups chicken broth
1 tsp thyme	2 Tbsp fresh oregano diced
1 cup rice milk	2 Tbsp cornstarch
1/2 tsp no-salt gravy-coloring liquid	2 Tbsp local honey
½ cup Irish whiskey	½ cup Madeira or Port wine
3 Tbsp EV olive oil	1 tsp ground black pepper

Start the brown sauce first. Sauté half the minced garlic in a pan with 1 tablespoon of olive oil; add thyme and half the oregano, as well as the honey. Cook until residue in pan is well darkened. Add another tablespoon olive oil and stir in the cornstarch until it, too, is brown; gradually add rice milk while stirring, and then the Madeira wine with the gravy coloring drops. When nicely thickened, set aside in a warmer-oven at 170 degrees.

Place the fillets of monkfish in a ceramic or glass baking dish with the two cups fat-free chicken broth. Brush the tops of the fish with one tablespoon of olive oil. Spread on top of the fish the remaining minced garlic plus the black pepper, and two thin slices of lemon. Pour the Irish whiskey over the fish. Bake in a moderate oven, 300 degrees, for 40 minutes. Place the fillets of monkfish in a shallow concave serving dish. Mix the remaining liquid from the baking dish into the set-aside sauce and stir all together well.

Pour this semi-thick brown sauce all around the monkfish (not on top) and serve up with spinach and squash. Decorate with lemon wedges.

Juan's Kitchen

www.juanswellness.com

http://superseniorswellness.blogspot.com/

Photos by Maggie Conley on covers and page 100 & 139. Photos by Ellen Warfield on page 106, 100, and Juan's picture on page 136. Other photos taken by O'Callahan family members.

Made in the USA
Charleston, SC
16 November 2012